KIDS EXPLORE
THE HERITAGE OF
WESTERN NATIVE AMERICANS

Westridge Young Writers Workshop

John Muir Publications
Santa Fe, New Mexico

When you read this book you will learn
All kinds of people make the world turn.
Each is different in his or her own way,
We want you to know that that's okay.
These heroes have taught us things we didn't know,
Now along with us you can grow.

John Muir Publications, P.O. Box 613, Santa Fe, NM 87504
© 1995 by Jefferson County School District N. R-1
Cover © 1995 John Muir Publications
All rights reserved. Published 1995
Printed in the United States of America

First edition.　　First printing July 1995
　　　　　　　　　First TWG printing July 1995

Library of Congress Cataloging-in-Publication Data
Kids explore the heritage of western Native Americans / Westridge Young Writers
　Workshop. — 1st ed.
　p.　　cm.
　Includes index.
　ISBN 1-56261-189-5 (pbk.)
　1. Indians of North America—West (U.S.)—Juvenile literature.　2. West (U.S.)—
History—Juvenile literature.　3. Children's writings, American.　I. Westridge
　Young Writers Workshop.
E78.W5K53　　1995
978'.00497—dc20　　　　　　　　　　　　　　　　　95-16767
　　　　　　　　　　　　　　　　　　　　　　　　　　　CIP
　　　　　　　　　　　　　　　　　　　　　　　　　　　AC

Production: Kathryn Lloyd-Strongin, Sarah Johansson
Design: Susan Surprise
Typesetting: Marcie Pottern
Printer: Malloy Lithographing, Inc.

Distributed to the book trade by
Publishers Group West
Emeryville, California

Distributed to the education trade by
Wright Group Publishing, Inc.
19201 120th Avenue NE
Bothell, WA 98011

CONTENTS

ACKNOWLEDGMENTS

When you turn the pages of this book,
Open your mind and take a good look.
Native Americans are here today,
Living all around you in a modern way.
These families' stories are no longer a mystery,
They are more than a part of America's history.
Remember, the earth would be a better place,
If we respect the traditions of every race.

We, the young authors who helped write *Kids Explore the Heritage of Western Native Americans,* have learned so much from working and writing together. Some of us live on reservations, some of us live in the country, some of us live in small towns, and some of us live in cities. We really appreciate all the people who helped us. We would not have been able to tell the stories of the families without their cooperation and patience. We want to thank all the volunteers who contributed. Here are the names of some of the people who helped make this book possible.

Richard Begay
Stephanie Berryhill
Aaron Brenne
George Christe
Dr. Rosalin Clark
Alan Cook
Jim Craig
Jeff Danos
Wayne Dennis
Denver Public Library
Dr. Alan Downer
Victor Devill
Debbie Echohawk
Darryl Etchison
Tricia Fleury
Shannon Gash
Terry Gray

Dr. Willard Gilbert
Darlene H. Hallam
Roger Hartstone
Dr. Karen Harvey
Daisy Herodes
Kathy Herodes
Ron Horn
Leigh Jenkins
Sandy Kiona
J.P. Knox
Rose Lee
Kenneth Morphet-Brown
Brycene A. Neaman
Leslie Nelson
Peter Noyes
Paula Oliver
Sue Rivgon

Rose Roy
Linda S. Salazar
Gloria Sho-Walter
Lisa Skidmore
Courtney Smith
Dee Smith
Marian Stewart
Nicole Taylor
Dr. Leola Taylor
Gilbert Timeche
Evelyn Thomas
Tim Thompson
Jolena Tillequots
Rachele Vaughan
Ruth Van Otten
Wapato Indian Club
B.J. War Club

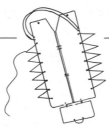

STUDENTS' PREFACE

Dear Reader,

This book tells the story of six Native American individuals and their families. Each family was recommended by people of their own Indian nation. In our book, you will discover the differences and similarities among them.

We would like you to understand why we chose to write about these wonderful people. They are all unique. They are challenged in different ways and they all have overcome struggles. Some of them live in big cities and others live in small towns or in the country. Some live on reservations. Some of them have big families, while other families are very small. Some of these people work for public or private schools. One is a judge, one owns her own company, and another helps people start businesses of their own. One person is even the principal chief of his nation. All of the families are respected and loved. They have all shared their stories to help us understand what they believe.

Though very different, these families are also alike in many ways. They are all striving to keep their heritage alive while helping to make our country a better place. In this way, the people featured in our book are like the pieces of a multicolored quilt. They are different parts of a pattern that fit together to make a beautiful world.

TEACHERS' PREFACE

We accept the challenge of building a brighter future.
We will not ignore the problems caused by racism in America.
We pledge to continue to work for respect for all Americans.

The fifth book in the Kids Explore series, *Kids Explore the Heritage of Western Native Americans,* is a product of the Westridge Young Writers Workshop. Although the workshop is located at Westridge Elementary in Jefferson County, Colorado, students from all around the country write for this program. Classrooms and teachers throughout the United States have worked together to prepare the chapters of this book. Sometimes half of a chapter was done in one location, such as on a reservation, and the other half in another locale.

We have chosen to use young writers because students are interested in what their peers think and see. *Kids Explore the Heritage of Western Native Americans* was written during one school year with the participation of 300 Native American and non-Native American students and teachers from five states: Arizona, Colorado, Oklahoma, Washington, and Wyoming. The

authors are students in the third through seventh grades.

There are more than 500 Native American groups, or nations, in the United States today. This book can cover only a few. We have chosen six Indian nations from the western and midwestern part of our country and hope to talk about others in later editions of this book. (For purposes of sentence flow, we have used the terms Native American, American Indian, and Indian interchangeably, although Native American is the preferred usage.) If you know of someone who might be interested in taking part in a future project, please contact John Muir Publications.

For each tribal heritage we talk about people, customs, history, folktales, food, and fun. Each family in this book belongs to a different Native American nation. Remember, though, that they are telling their own family's story and do not necessarily represent all people within their nation.

When we started researching this book, we found history books on Native Americans to be plentiful. However, the history was often told from a non-Indian point of view, so we have included each nation's perspective in their chapter timeline. We were surprised that we did not find many books presenting an accurate picture of modern Native American families. So we decided that the focus of this book should be American Indian families of today.

It was astounding to discover that the majority of public school students to whom we sent questionnaires had no knowledge of current Native American families, but only of their past history. It was also disheartening to find that many responses revealed a belief in stereotypes and myths about American Indians. The goal of this book is to make future generations aware that Native Americans are active in today's society and making contributions for a stronger America. We challenge children, adults, and teachers to break the cycle of stereotyped characterizations and spread an accurate picture of Native American families today.

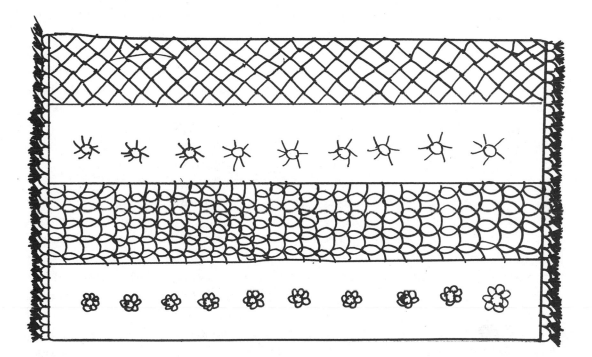

INTRODUCTION

Sometimes people wonder who discovered America. We don't think we will ever really know. Although many native tribes have lived in America for hundreds of years, no one really knows how the first people came here.

Several million people lived in North America before the arrival of Europeans. These people believed the land belonged to the Creator, and they tried to use it in wise ways. Some groups were hunters and others were farmers. The hunters moved across the land killing only the animals they needed for food, tools, clothing, and shelter. They didn't say the land was theirs. The land was for everyone to use and share.

Before Europeans came to this country, the people who lived here called themselves by the name of their tribes. For example, if you met a farmer in the Southwest and asked him what he was, he might have said, "I am a Hopi," or just called himself one of "the People." When Europeans first came to America, they found hundreds of tribes here already. It wasn't until Columbus arrived and thought he was in India that the word "Indian" was used for all tribes. Even though the Indians were scattered all over the country, spoke different languages, and had different customs, they were all given the same name. It seems strange to us that this happened.

Life was hard for the Indians after the Europeans came. The Europeans brought many sicknesses with them that the Indians had never had. They wanted to take over and claim the riches of the "new" land. Many Europeans tried to change the Indians and take away their freedom. The Spanish wanted to convert the Indians to Christianity and use them to do their work. They tried to get the Indians to live in one place. The French trappers and traders wanted to use the Indians to help them get more animal skins to sell.

The British passed laws that said no one could take the Indians' land. In 1763, the British ruled that the land west of the Appalachian Mountains belonged to the Indians. People obeyed this law until the United States passed the Indian Removal Act of 1830. Then the government started moving the Indians off their land and giving the land to white settlers. Things would never be the same again for the Indians. The Indians would be given different land until gold or something else of value was discovered; then the government and settlers would find another way to seize the land again. Treaties or agreements were made, but the treaties were usually broken, most often by white people.

The U.S. government continued to pass laws that changed the lives of Native Americans. In the late 1800s most Indians were forced to live on reservations. Reservations are pieces of land that have been set aside for the different tribes. Today there are hundreds of reservations located in 34 states. Reservations do not belong to the U.S. government. Sometimes two or three tribes live on one reservation. The Shoshone and Arapaho, for example, share the Wind River Reservation in Wyoming. Even if they used to be enemies, now they are expected to get along with one another. Sometimes a tribe's reservation is far away from where their people used to live. This means that these tribes have had to change some of their customs and traditions because things are different in their new location.

Through these struggles, the tribal governments changed, too. In the past, each tribe had its own government and legal systems, and dealt with other tribes on its own. But when they had to move to reservations and obey the U.S. government's laws, the tribes lost a lot of their power. Today they can't make their own treaties and must ask the U.S. government for permission to do things like sell land.

The different tribes or nations have worked hard to get back as much of their power as possible. They have written laws and rules for the people in their nations to follow, and they run their own governments. They have different kinds of leadership. Some have councils that run their business. Some councils are elected, and some have their elders, the older respected leaders, choose the members. Other tribes have one leader. These leaders are called different names like chairman, president, or principal chief. These governments do different things just like the U.S. government. There are many books you can read if you are interested in how tribal governments work.

In 1924, the Snyder Act made all Native Americans citizens of the U.S. Since then they have been members of two groups, and have rights and responsibilities to both of their governments. As citizens of the United States, they vote, pay taxes, and can serve in the military. As citizens of their tribal nations, they take part in their tribal government and can live on or off their tribal lands.

We have shared the stories of six families from different Indian nations in the western part of the United States: the Muscogee (Creek), Arapaho, Navajo, Hopi, Yakama, and Sioux Nations. Each chapter includes the family's story, an overview of the tribe's traditional culture, a historical timeline of the tribe, information about customs, traditional stories, recipes, games, and crafts, and a letter from the authors that shares the vision they have for the future. We hope our book will help you learn more about modern Native Americans and break the stereotypes people have about them.

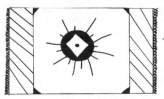

EXPLORING THE
MUSCOGEE (CREEK) HERITAGE
WITH PRINCIPAL CHIEF BILL FIFE

The Fife family believes in education and staying in school,
A close, caring family that lives by the Golden Rule.
They have many hopes and strong beliefs,
That is why one of them is the nation's chief.

 We would like you to meet a special family, the Fife family. They are members of the Muscogee (Creek) Nation. The tribe has two names because the name they use for themselves and the name they were given by the U.S. government are different. The traditional Muscogee people often lived near creeks and streams, so the first white people who met them called them "Creeks." Today, the people call themselves the Muscogee (Creek). Here is the story of one Muscogee (Creek) family.

PRINCIPAL CHIEF BILL FIFE'S STORY

There was a large crowd watching the inaugural day celebration in Okmulgee, Oklahoma on January 4, 1992. More than 100 members of the Fife family were there to share the honor as Bill Fife was sworn in as the principal chief of the Muscogee (Creek) Nation. The new chief and his family and many other Muscogee people had worked hard to make this dream come true.

The first time Bill Fife ran for chief, the Fife family helped with the campaign, made posters, and did everything they could to help him win. Then, on election night they had a watch party and everyone stayed up and waited to see who won the election. That time, Bill did not win, but the Fife family did not give up.

The next time Bill ran for chief, everyone worked even harder. Bill's sisters and his friends used what they knew about art to make campaign signs. His brothers, sisters, and other supporters helped Muscogee people find the right forms and sign up to vote. They also arranged rides for people to the voting places. Children wore Musco-

Hon. Glen D. Johnson (left), speaker, Oklahoma House of Representatives, congratulates Principal Chief Bill S. Fife on Inauguration Day

gee clothes and rode in parades all over Muscogee land. One night all the kids stayed up until three in the morning helping the adults get letters ready to send to voters.

The night of the election, the Fifes had another watch party and many Muscogee people came. This time Bill won, and everyone was so happy. Bill Fife was now principal chief of the Muscogee Nation, which is something like being president of the United States.

It is a Muscogee custom that when someone in the family does something well, the whole family is honored. So Jim Fife, the chief's father, and all the other Fifes stood in a half-circle and shook hands with the people at the party accepting their best wishes. The Fifes were proud of their

family and proud of their Muscogee heritage. Because the Fife family really made us believe that a family can always stick together and help each other, we are going to tell you their story.

THE FAMILY

This family's story starts with the birth of James Fife, a full-blood Muscogee (Creek) and father of Principal Chief Fife. James Fife was born on March 28, 1904, in the Muscogee Nation, Indian Territory, which later became part of the state of Oklahoma. He was born into the bear clan. His family and friends called him Jimmie or Jim. Soon after he was born, Jim received his own piece of land (called an allotment) from the government. Jim grew up in the house on his family's land and became a citizen of the United States in 1924, when Congress gave citizenship to all Indians.

In 1937, Jim married Willia Carmen Griffin, a member of the raccoon clan and almost one half Muscogee. They had nine children, all members of the raccoon clan, since by custom all Mus-

cogee children belong to their mother's clan. Their first daughter, Hannah, died right after birth, and they didn't know why. The rest of the Fife children were all healthy. Both Mr. and Mrs. Fife had gone to college, and they encouraged their children to get good educations, join clubs and athletic teams, and become leaders. Mr. Fife's motto was always, "Be strong in mind and body." Both parents were good role models for their children. In 1986, Mrs. Fife was named Oklahoma Indian Mother of the Year.

Jim and Carmen Fife, and most of their family, attend an all-day meeting at the Thlewarle (pronounced "thle-wa-thle") Indian Baptist Church on the fourth Sunday of each month. Their church is almost like a camp because 11 cabins, called camphouses, surround the churchhouse. Because church services last all day and on into the evening families go back to their camphouses and serve meals. Visitors are always welcome at all camphouses and are not expected to bring food. When church is ready to begin again, the church deacon blows a horn called Pofketv (bof-kih-duh), inviting all families and their visitors back for the services. The ceremonies and singing are mostly in the Muscogee language.

Because most of their family has gone to this church for over 100 years, this church is very special to the Fife family. Jim Fife was baptized here, like most of the other Fife family members. Jim's father, Sunday Fife, served as the pastor of Thlewarle Indian Baptist Church, and his grandfather, Kenucke Low, helped start the church. The Lows were from old Thlewarle Tribal Town.

Some of Mr. and Mrs. Fife's children and grandchildren take part in ceremonial dances, a practice of the traditional Muscogee religion. These dances take place throughout the spring and summer months, at the traditional ceremonial grounds within the Muscogee Nation. Each ceremonial ground was once the center of a tribal town. Each contains a square for official meetings, ceremonial dances, and traditional activities. An area next to the square is reserved for playing stickball, a traditional game of the Muscogee people. Family camps, arranged by clan, surround the square. The arrangement and purpose of camp houses at the Muscogee churches is similar to that of the traditional ceremonial grounds.

Grandkids Derek, Lisa, and Brandy Fife were reared in the traditional Muscogee religion of their mother. Derek is becoming a ceremonial dance leader, and his sisters were taught to be shell shakers by their Grandma Bear. They are members of the Hickory Ground Ceremonial Ground.

Art has always been important to the Fife family. When the children were young, they would all watch their mother work on quilts and other artwork. Their father, a skilled craftsman, made his wife's wedding ring and later made spurs for his son Bill. For each one of the girls in the family, he made a bead loom. Carmen Fife taught the kids how to use pokeberry juice and other natural plants for dyes. They dug for clay on the creek banks to make pottery and sculpture. Although the children didn't have as many toys as kids have today, they

Jimmie (Carole) Fife

"The Earth is Our Mother"

had a lot of natural supplies, and most of their toys were handmade.

When Jimmie Carole, the oldest daughter, was nine, she started collecting pictures of the Plains Indians from cereal boxes. She collected these cards for a long time, because she knew that someday they might come in handy. And they did!

One day, her family put up brand new, light peach colored wallpaper in the kitchen. It looked great, but after the family went to bed, Jimmie Carole tiptoed to the kitchen with her picture cards. She started drawing a mural all over the new wallpaper. Jimmie Carole worked all night long, copying the pictures off her cards. When she was done, there were pictures of the daily life of the Plains Indians all over the kitchen wall. It looked terrific.

The next morning, when Jimmie Carole's mom saw the mural, she wasn't mad like some parents would have been. Instead, she told Carole the mural was very nice, and she left the mural up for years to come. When Jimmie Carole was older, she painted a mural for the city of Seattle, Washington. We wonder if they know it was actually Jimmie Carole's second mural!

Jimmie Carole's sisters are artists, too. Phyllis is a painter and designer. Sandy paints, weaves, and does beadwork. Robin does sign painting and graphics, and Sharon designs and writes. In fact, at one time, the Fife sisters owned a designer clothing store, called the Fife Collection, in Henryetta, Oklahoma. Their business logo, or design, was the raccoon, which represented their Muscogee clan.

The Fifes do a lot of things together in Dustin, Oklahoma. In the summer of 1976, the town held its first Spokogee celebration with a parade, a rodeo, and games. (Spokogee is the town's original Indian name.) Jim Fife asked his grandchildren to be in the parade, and because they would never refuse their grandpa, they said yes. Four of them had just learned to walk, but they went, too. The whole Fife gang dressed up and marched down Main Street, which is just a couple of blocks long. The Fifes have been going to the Spokogee celebration ever since. They've won many prizes in the parades, and had fun at the frog races and the calf scrambles at the rodeo. At one of the Spokogee celebrations, Jim Fife was honored as a community elder by the town of Dustin.

One year Jim Fife bought a raffle ticket for a quarter and won a little pig. He named it Miss Pig. When they were trying to put Miss Pig into her cage, she got away. The kids all chased her and caught her and took her home. Everyone adored Miss Pig, but as time went on, Miss Pig grew to weigh about a half-ton (1,000 pounds)! The uncles built her a big pig house with a cloth door. Miss Pig loved to have the grandkids come scratch her back with sticks and bring her treats. One morning when the grandkids were eating with Grandpa Jim, he held up some bacon and said, "It's about time for Miss Pig to be bacon."

The kids all said, "No, no, we can't eat our friend!" So instead of making her into bacon, Grandpa Jim sold Miss Pig. After she was gone, the grandchildren often went to the pigpen and talked about her a lot.

Grandpa and Grandma Fife had 21 grandchildren, and we are going to talk about two of them, Sharry and James. Sharry helped us write this chapter, and James is named after his Grandpa Jim Fife. Sharry is the daughter of Sharon Fife-Mouss and Ed Mouss. She is almost a full-blooded Indian. Sharry has long dark brown hair, brown eyes, and wears glasses. She attends Henryetta Elementary in Henryetta, Oklahoma where she is the secretary of her fourth grade class.

Sharry is friendly, smart, and always quiet. She has lots of friends, probably because she is nice. She never has trouble turning in her work on time, and she gets good grades. If someone makes a joke, she laughs, even if it's not so funny. When someone needs help, she is ready to help any time.

We were lucky Sharry was in our class. If she hadn't been, we wouldn't have made Indian fry bread or tried straw weaving. If you want to weave, look in the crafts section for how to do it. Sharry is very proud of her Muscogee heritage and has started entering her art and weavings in competitions, so she can share them with others.

Sharry Fife-Mouss

Fourth-grader James Fife is ten years old and lives in Dustin, Oklahoma. He has won many awards and trophies for both art and sports. He plays basketball (his jersey number is 55), likes football and wrestling, and once built a small wrestling ring in his own yard. James collects baseball caps, and has a football card signed by quarterback Jim Kelly of the Buffalo Bills.

When James Fife gave us a videotape tour of the farm he lives on, he showed us an old house that sits in a grove of trees. It was about 100 years old and pretty worn down. No one lives in the house anymore, but

James likes living on the farm near the old house, because that is where Grandpa Jim was born.

James is proud to have his grandpa's name and to have shared so many wonderful experiences with him. James and his grandpa enjoyed planting gardens together. They grew lots of potatoes, corn, okra, tomatoes, and many other vegetables.

For each grandchild, Grandpa Jim always planted a special tree, and he wanted James to have a tree all his own too. So Grandpa Jim took James down to Taylor's Bottom,

James Fife

which belonged to Grandpa Jim's brother Taylor Fife, and found just the right tree. They dug it out of the ground, carried it off in the trunk of their car, then planted it in their yard. James' tree is a wild plum tree, about six feet tall now. It blossoms every spring and will have fruit this year.

James remembers how Grandpa Jim liked to fix things, too. Once he found an old bat that had been broken on the end and decided to fix it by carving a whole new end with rounded edges. At the time, James was too little to use a regular bat, but this bat was just his size. James saved this bat and has put his grandpa's name on it to help him remember his grandpa.

James' grandpa died in January of 1994. This was a very sad time for all of the Fifes, but they stuck together. Even though they miss him, the Fifes will never forget what Grandpa Jim taught them about life and learning.

That's why they wished he could have been with them when most of the Fife family drove two hours from Oklahoma to Arkansas University for Phyllis Fife's graduation. She had earned her doctorate degree. When Phyllis came across the stage, the whole Fife family cheered. The person who handed her the diploma said it was the biggest cheer there. Two other Fifes graduated the same year. Sharon Fife-Mouss got her master's degree from Oklahoma State University, and Jeff Fife graduated from the Oklahoma Law Enforcement Academy. He is a Muscogee Nation Lighthorse police officer. We think

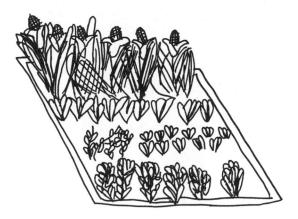

the Fifes will be going to a lot more graduations in the future.

Jim and Carmen Fife's Children

This is what Jim and Carmen Fife's children might be doing, if you met them today.

Jimmie Carole Fife, who goes by Carole, would be teaching fourth grade at Washington Elementary in Washington, Oklahoma. She is a graduate of Oklahoma State University and a well-known artist. Carole is married to Robert Stewart, a Chickasaw, and they have two children named Kelley and Maya. Kelley is married to Lonnie Ray Hyde and has two children of her own, Ashley and Colton. Maya, a high school freshman, has won many art awards in state-wide competitions and hopes to go to college like her sister did.

Principal Chief Bill Fife would probably be found in Okmulgee, Oklahoma, at the Muscogee Nation Tribal Complex. Before he became chief, Bill sat on the Muscogee Tribal Council and worked for the U.S. Postal Service. Bill is a veteran of the armed forces and served in the Vietnam War. He is married to Mary Nell Poe, a Chickasaw, and they have two children— Jeff, a Lighthorseman for the Muscogee Nation Police, and Cinda, a college student. Chief Fife is someone who really believes in helping people, and he is doing just that in the office of principal chief.

Sharon Fife-Mouss can be found at Oklahoma State University—Okmulgee, where she teaches communications and technical writing classes. She has helped write several books. Sharon and her husband, Edward, have three children and a grandchild, Damon. Lea and Eddie are in college, and Sharry is in fourth grade.

Phyllis Fife can be found at Northeastern State University in Tahlequah, Oklahoma, where she directs bilingual education training for teachers of Muscogee and Cherokee children. She has three daughters, Staci, Yahnah, and Shelley Patrick. Staci is in college, Yahnah in high school, and Shelley in middle school. Phyllis keeps very busy with art and community work. Her art is shown in many museums and books.

Sandy Fife Wilson teaches art at Morris Public School. Her art has been displayed all over the country. Sandy and her husband, Alfred Wilson, who is also a Muscogee, have three children, Laura, 12, Clinton, 10, and Daniel, 8. Sandy is a college graduate and attended an art institute. She wants her children to get a good education and has encouraged them to do art work. Her children have won many art awards. Sandy and her family are involved in many school and community activities.

If you were to try to find Tim Fife, he would probably be at a rodeo or ball game with his brothers, or tending horses at the family farm. Tim is a master mechanic with an associate's degree from Oklahoma State University Technical Branch. You might also find him at Muscogee Tribal Committee meetings, serving on the Muscogee Nation Legislative Council. When he ran for this office, he promised he would work to improve health care and develop the Muscogee community. He is married to Sheila Pendley. Their daughter, Tracy, is a freshman in college.

Brian Fife spends his time as a master mechanic at Ruth Motors in Henryetta, Oklahoma. Brian has served on the school board and on the Indian Parents' Committee where his kids go to school. Brian is married to Ila Bear, a full-blooded Muscogee and granddaughter of former Muscogee Chief Turner Bear. They have three children, Derek, Brandy, and Lisa, and a granddaughter named Sierra. Derek goes to Bacone College. Sophomore Brandy and eighth-grader Lisa both attend Dustin Public School.

Robin Fife could be found working on her master's degree and teaching art at Dustin Elementary. When her father Jim Fife was older and needed care, Robin gave up her job and she and her son James moved in to help him. She found work near their home and took care of him until he died in 1994. Robin is active in local organizations and the Dustin Muscogee Community.

Uncle Brian gives James some roping tips

Now you know who the Fifes are!

Fife Family Personal Statement

It is good that our family belongs to the great Muscogee nation of people. As children of Jim and Carmen Fife, we were brought up to know our heritage and to live within the culture of our tribe. As we grew up, this knowledge helped us to become who we are in heart and mind. But that was not all. We were helped to strengthen our minds with learning and our bodies with work and play. We were encouraged to learn and to expand our talents in clubs

Crosier's Studio

Front, left to right: Dr. Phyllis Fife, Jimmie Carole Fife Stewart, Sharon Mouss, Sandy Wilson. Back: Tim Fife, Principal Chief Bill Fife, James Fife, Robin Fife, and Brian Fife.

and organizations, and on teams, inside and outside school. We were inspired to travel when we had the chance and to learn about other people and places.

To nourish our spiritual lives, our family gave us the freedom to take part in the traditional Muscogee religion or the Christian church. We learned to follow the Creator's teaching, to show gratitude and respect for what we have, and to live a good and law-abiding life. We learned to think things through, to honor and respect family and friends, to be sensitive to the feelings of others, and to help those in need. We learned to surround ourselves with people who love us and whom we love in return, and to be loyal.

This is our background, and this is what we wish to pass on to our own families. A very simple Muscogee custom passed on in our family, from birth to death, is the handshake. The handshake is used everywhere to say hello or goodbye, as well as to offer peace, goodwill, agreement, and respect, among Muscogee people. The handshake might be one of the first gestures a baby learns. And in death, the final handshake is given by dropping a handful of dirt into the grave. From the Fife family to the children who read our story, we hope that you will help us keep the handshake alive.

THE MUSCOGEE (CREEK) NATION

The Muscogee (Creek) once lived in what is now Georgia and Alabama. The British settlers began calling the Muscogee "Creeks," because they lived in villages by the streams or creeks. The Muscogee were mostly hunters and farmers and used the water from the creeks for their crops. They grew maize (a type of corn), beans, squash, and pumpkins. They also hunted and fished for other food.

The Muscogee looked out for one another and usually kept some extra food to share with the needy. Many small tribes nearby had problems with the Europeans and came to the Muscogee for protection. They all worked together to form strong bonds with each other. The Spanish, the British, and the French all tried to work with the Muscogee, because these nations wanted the Muscogee land and were planning to have it.

The Muscogee's winter homes were made of bark or grass and had a place for a fire in the middle. There were no windows and only a small door. During the

MUSCOGEE (CREEK) NATION

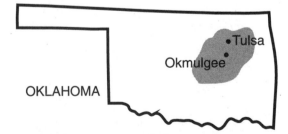

There is no official Muscogee (Creek) reservation. The Muscogee (Creek) Nation is centered in north-central Oklahoma. Okmulgee is the capital of the Muscogee (Creek) Nation.

summer, the Muscogee lived in long buildings that also had a place for a fire in the middle. The summer houses were very open and had no walls. The straw roof kept the hot sun out. In the middle area, the children played and people got together. Each group of families, called a clan, lived together in tribal towns. Members of each clan worked hard and took care of each other. All clans had names like raccoon, or bear, or wind.

The Muscogee people lived in tribal towns. Each town had its own government but met with other tribal towns to make decisions that would include everyone. Each town had its own ceremonial ground where spiritual ceremonies and meetings were held. Over the years, missionaries worked in some of these tribal towns. When the Muscogee had to move from their homelands to the Indian Territory (now Oklahoma), the tribal towns were started again. Some towns established their own Christian churches and included many traditional Indian customs and beliefs.

Today there are about 35,000 Muscogee living in east-central Oklahoma. The Muscogee have one of the most organized governments in the state. Their leaders meet and work with the Cherokee, Choctaw, Chickasaw, and Seminole tribes in Oklahoma.

The Muscogee are committed to carrying on their way of life. Fifteen traditional ceremonial grounds are still active. Ceremonies are held every year in the spring and the fall. These ceremonies are a special time of fasting and cleansing, and are celebrated with dancing, eating, and playing stickball. The Green Corn Ceremony, one of the best known celebrations, is held every year after harvest time to give thanks for the earth's abundance.

CUSTOMS AND TRADITIONS

Green Corn Ceremony

Many ancient Muscogee customs are still followed today. One of these customs is Posketv (bos-kih-duh), the Green Corn Ceremony. Posketv is a very old and important celebration near harvest time for corn. For four days, on the ceremonial grounds of their nation, the Muscogee give thanks for their corn, which they call the grain of life.

To prepare for the celebration, men drink a special tea made from holly leaves to purify themselves, and perform many dances. They will sing all during the celebrations. The women dance and shake their shells in a special dance called the "Ribbon Dance." The dancers offer prayers of thanks to the Creator for the gift of past crops and ask to be blessed with good future crops. The dancing and singing never stop, even at night. At certain times in between the dances, young boys receive the names they will be called as adults.

The end of the four-day celebration marks the beginning of the new year. After the celebration, the men scatter the ashes from the ceremonial fire and they build a New Year's fire. This wonderful celebration is usually held in July or August.

HISTORY TIMELINE

Before 1500 The Muscogee (Creek) lived in what is today the southeastern United States. Early ancestors of the Muscogee built great earth mounds at their ceremonial centers near the rivers. Later they established tribal towns near these same rivers.

1540 Spanish explorers, led by Hernando de Soto, invaded the Muscogee's land. At this time, there were about six or seven Muscogee groups with their own governments.

1600s The Muscogee began trading with the British, French, and Spanish.

1690 By 1690, the Muscogee tribes had joined together to form a confederacy, which was called the best political organization north of Mexico. As the Europeans devastated small tribes, more of them joined the Muscogee Creek Confederacy.

1813-14 The Muscogee Indian War began and ended. Some Muscogee called the Red Stick Prophets, who followed traditional Indian ways, began fighting with other Muscogee who didn't follow Indian ways. Americans called this the Red Stick War.

1814 General Andrew Jackson and his troops invaded Muscogee land. William McIntosh and his followers sided with Jackson and the U.S. troops. Finally, the Red Sticks and the traditional Musco-gee were defeated at the Battle of Horse-shoe Bend. The Muscogee signed the Treaty of Fort Jackson.

1825 William McIntosh signed the Treaty of Indian Springs that sold all Muscogee land in Georgia and a small strip in Alabama to the U.S. government. He did this against Muscogee Council orders. Later, William McIntosh was executed because he betrayed the laws of the confederacy. The treaty was soon voted out, because it was not signed by all the tribal officials.

1826 The Treaty of Washington was signed by official Muscogee leaders. This treaty gave up Georgia lands but kept Alabama homelands. The Muscogee were the only nation to force the U.S. government to tear up a treaty.

1827 The Muscogee, who had been under McIntosh's leadership, resettled in Indian Territory.

1832 Once again, the U.S. government wanted more land. The Removal Treaty of 1832 forced the Muscogee people to move west of the Mississippi to an area called Indian Territory. The U.S. promised the Muscogee Indians that they could rule themselves and that there would never be a state on Indian lands.

1836-37 The rest of the Muscogee people were forced to move from the southeastern homelands to a new location in

Indian Territory. On the journey west, many people died from drowning, sickness, and freezing.

1867 Even though the Muscogee were forced to relocate, they reorganized as the Muscogee Nation.

1887 The General Allotment, or Dawes Act, was passed by the U.S. government. Before this act, the land belonged to the whole Muscogee Nation. This act took the land and divided it into individual allotments, so that each family got up to 160 acres. This act paved the way for Oklahoma to become a state. In previous treaties, the government had promised that the land would belong to the Muscogee forever, and no state would be built on land owned by tribes. Once again, the government broke a promise.

1898 The Curtis Act took away the tribal courts and required all laws passed by the tribal government to be okayed by the president of the United States. Even the chief was to be appointed by the president.

1907 Members of the Five Tribes, including the Muscogee, tried to establish an Indian state called Sequoyah. They wrote a state constitution, passed it, and sent it to the U.S. Congress. Congress ignored it and instead allowed Oklahoma to become a state.

1900-01 Chitto Harjo tried to keep the Muscogee Nation government together as the U.S. government tried to do away with it.

1934 The Oklahoma Indian Welfare Act was passed. This gave the Muscogee a chance to reorganize their tribal government with the purchase of land for their government headquarters. This act made some good changes for the Muscogee.

1971 The U. S. government gave the Muscogee Nation permission to elect a principal chief.

1979 The new constitution of the Muscogee Nation, first proposed in 1975, was approved by election.

1980s The U.S. Supreme Court said that the Muscogee government was its own nation with rights to tribal courts and taxes like any other nation.

1992 Bill Fife was elected principal chief.

Today The Muscogee have never had a reservation. The only tribal land they have is used for the capital complex, a few businesses, health care centers, and housing. Many Muscogee work in cities and on farms. The Muscogee Nation is working hard for a good future.

Stomp Dances

The stomp dances are a part of Muscogee traditional religion and a form of traditional dancing. Sometimes a small hand rattle of traditional turtle shells is used for the dance.

Traditional turtle shells are are worn only by women, and they are hard to make. Once the turtle meat is removed from the shell, holes are drilled into the shell to let the sound come through. The shells are filled with small rocks and then closed up to make them rattle. Women wear the turtle shells fastened to their legs with leather straps or strong bootlaces.

Some Muscogee now use small milk cans instead of turtle shells. The milk cans make a sound different from the traditional turtle shells, and the turtle shells are preferred.

Because these ceremonial dances have a special religious meaning to the people, they are not tourist attractions.

Damon Mouss at 4 months, with his head shaved in the Creek tradition (except for a Mohawk-style strip)

Head Shaving

Among all the many different customs in the Muscogee tradition, one is just for babies. When a baby is four months old, it is the tradition to shave off all the baby's hair. The Fife family has always done this and believe that the hair is nicer when it grows back. Sometimes when they shave the baby's head, they will leave one strip of hair at the top of the head just like a Mohawk cut. The newest Fife baby, Damon, just received his special haircut from his father.

Funerals

When someone from the Thlewarle Indian Baptist Church dies, a deacon will go to the churchhouse and blow on the horn four times. This is what happened when Jim Fife died. His body was placed in an open casket at the Thlewarle Indian Baptist Church, where his family and other church members held a wake service. A wake is a lot like a last visit with someone who has died. Family members sit all night long near the open casket, remembering all the happy moments they shared together.

About a thousand people came to Grandpa Jim's funeral the next day. He was honored with many Muscogee songs and prayers. After the funeral, his casket was taken to the family cemetery, covered with a family quilt, and put into the ground while a prayer was said. Everyone took a handful of dirt and threw it into his grave for their final handshake with Grandpa Jim.

Most Muscogee families have their own cemetery on a piece of land near their home. Grandpa Fife's body was buried in the family cemetery only a mile from his home. A little house called a gravehouse was placed over his grave. The gravehouse is about four feet tall and has a little window on the west end, for the spirit to come and go. The body is placed facing the east, because that is where the sun comes up, and Christians believe that is where Christ will appear again.

When gravehouses get old, families don't repair them, because they believe the house is always new to the spirit, even when it is old and worn out in the world. Sometimes Muscogee who don't have family graveyards can be buried in a corner of another family's cemetery.

A gravehouse in the Fife family cemetery

Language

One of the first things the Fife children learn is how to count in Muscogee. Several Fife children have taken Muscogee language classes and learned to speak Muscogee from their grandparents. We wanted to share some words they use with you.

one — *hvmken* (huhm-gihn)
two — *hokkólen* (hohg-goh-lihn)
three — *tutcénen* (dood-jihn-ihn)
four — *osten* (ohs-dihn)
five — *cáhképen* (jah-gee-bihn)
six — *epáken* (ih-bah-gihn)
seven — *kulvpáken* (gool-uh-bah-gihn)
eight — *cenvpáken* (jih-nuh-bah-gihn)
nine — *ostvpáken* (oh-a-stuh-bah-gihn)
ten — *pálen* (bah-lin)
thank you — *mvtó* (muh-doh)

STORIES AND LEGENDS

Stories and legends are very important to the Muscogee. Some are used to teach lessons, and others are used to explain why something is the way it is. Here is a Muscogee story we have retold for you. We hope you will be able to tell which kind it is.

The Legend of the Woodpecker

Centuries ago, there was a woman who could bake bread far better than anyone else. Everybody knew her because she always wore a red bandana, a black dress, and a white apron.

One day, as she was sitting on her porch, she saw an old, ragged man step into her yard. "Do have any bread and water to spare for a hungry man?" he asked.

"You may get some water from the well and I will go find some bread," she told him.

The woman went inside to get some bread, but the only bread she had was too good to share with a ragged old man. So she decided to make a new loaf of bread. When it was done, it was even better than the first. So with the last of her flour she made another loaf. This turned out to be the best bread she had ever made! All of the bread she had made was far too good for a ragged old man.

The woman went outside and said to the man, "I'm sorry, but I guess I don't have any bread to give you after all." All of a sudden, the man began turning into a tall, well-dressed man. Too late, the woman realized this man was the Creator, He-sa-ke-ta-me-see. "Oh! Oh! I did not know it was you. If I had known, I would have given you the bread!"

"If your bread is too good for a poor, hungry old man, you are not worthy of your tal-ent," said He-sa-ke-ta-me-see. "From now on, you and your family will have to work hard for your food."

The woman's red bandana turned into red feathers, her black dress into black feathers, and her white apron into white feathers. As this happened, she began to shrink. Her feet became bird feet and her mouth changed into a beak. "Now you will have to peck trees for the food you eat," said He-sa-ke-ta-me-see.

That is how the woodpecker came to be.

FOOD AND FUN

Food and crafts are some of the things that connect the Muscogee with their relatives from long ago. Here are some foods and things to make that we thought you might have fun trying.

Blue Dumplings

The Fifes eat blue dumplings often. They taste good with black-eyed peas, beans, meat, or anything you might eat for dinner. They're really good for breakfast, too. Most Muscogee women know how to make them. Staci, who showed us how to cook them, learned how from her mother, Phyllis Fife, and her aunt, Sharon Fife-Mouss.

You will need:
2 cups of flour (We recommend Masa Harina flour, which is used to make corn tortillas. You can buy it in most large grocery stores.)

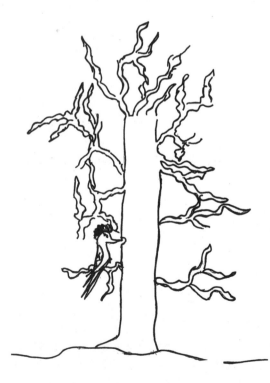

2 tablespoons of fine ashes from burnt pea hulls or corn shucks. (For variety, use 1 cup diced sweet potatoes or 1 cup cooked pinto beans instead of pea hull ashes.)

How to make pea hull or corn husk ashes:
Caution: This should be done outside, and with adult supervision.
Put about ½ bushel of dried pea hulls or corn husks in a large, clean metal pot or can. Light the hulls or husks with a match or piece of paper until they catch fire. Be careful; the fire could blaze high. Stir occasionally until all hulls have burned. Cool, then sift. Store in a large can with a lid.

How to make blue dumplings:
1. Put at least five inches of water into a pot and bring to a boil. The pot should be about two-thirds full.
2. Remember to wash your hands! Put the flour into a bowl.
3. Rub the ashes between your fingers and into the flour. This will make your fingers black, but don't worry—it will wash off.
4. Make a hole in the center of the flour and ashes. Find a cup with a handle and dip it into the boiling water. Be careful not to burn yourself. Pour the water into the bowl.
5. Use a big spoon to stir the water and flour mixture. Keep adding water and stirring until it looks and feels like crumbly clay.
6. Get a small bowl of cold water. Dip

Staci Fife Patrick helps the authors prepare blue dumplings

your hands into the cold water, so you don't burn yourself as you shape the mixture into patties the size of thick cookies.
7. Put the patties into the boiling water for 20-30 minutes.

Blue dumplings can be eaten in many ways. Some people like them with a half teaspoon of bacon grease (or any kind of grease from meat) and salt. Others like them with sugar. You can experiment with anything you know you like. If you have leftovers, you can slice and fry them.

Grape Dumplings
We learned how to make another recipe that is great for grape lovers!

You will need:
2 cups flour
½ cup sugar
1 quart grape juice from wild possum grapes (you may substitute grape juice from the store)

How to make grape dumplings:

1. Mix ¼ cup of the sugar with the flour in a bowl.
2. Mix ¼ cup of the sugar with the grape juice in a saucepan.
3. Heat juice mixture until it steams.
4. Measure ¼ cup of the juice mixture and pour it into the flour mixture.
5. Mix this into a thick dough while letting the rest of the juice come to a slow boil.
6. Sprinkle a little extra flour on a piece of waxed paper and pound or roll the dough on the waxed paper.
7. Make pieces about the size of a small cookie and drop them into the boiling juice.
8. Simmer about 30 minutes on low heat.

We know you will enjoy eating this Muscogee recipe, too. It is good when you serve it as dessert. It doesn't need to be hot or cold, just room temperature.

Straw Weaving

Weaving is something that many Native Americans do. The Muscogee had different ways of weaving that were hard to do, but we thought you would enjoy a much easier way of weaving. Straw weaving is easy when you get the hang of it, but you have to be patient to learn. The Fife children have enjoyed doing this activity over the years. The first time you try it, you might want to make a short weaving.

You will need:
yarn, cut into long pieces
scissors
rubber bands
drinking straws (Two or more, depending on how wide you want your weaving to be. Use a small number of straws for a thin weaving, more straws for a wider

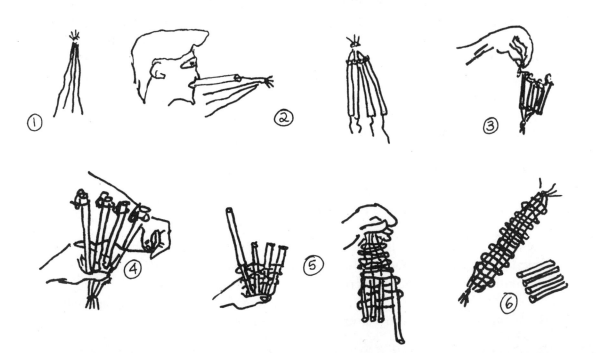

one. It is easier to weave with an even number. Use thick straws the first time.)

How to make a straw weaving:
1. Tie your yarn in a knot at one end.
2. Put one piece of yarn through each straw by sucking it—but watch out! If you suck too hard, you might get it in your mouth.
3. Wrap each end around your finger, then slip it off and put it against the straw. Wrap a rubber band around it.
4. Get a long piece of yarn and tie it above the knot at the bottom. Hold the bottom of the straws together. Start weaving it in and out of the straws. When the straws get full, pull up on the yarn at the top, and down on the yarn woven across the straws. This helps make the weaving longer than the straws.
5. When you want to change colors, tie another piece of yarn to the end of the yarn you were using. Keep on weaving.
6. When you have woven it long enough, take the straws out and tie the ends together in a knot like the one you made at the beginning.

We had a lot of fun doing this project. You might want to do a small one for a bracelet or headband until you get really good at it. Then you might make a belt.

Gorget
A gorget is a traditional neck decoration worn by Muscogee men.

They have neat designs. Some gorgets are made out of copper with designs hammered or shaped in them. Others are made out of shell with designs carved in them. We have drawn examples of Muscogee designs used on gorgets. The two dots at the top of most designs were holes for strings to tie around your neck.

You will need:
thick posterboard
white glue
heavy aluminum foil
permanent markers
hole puncher
scissors
2 feet of
   yarn
pen cap

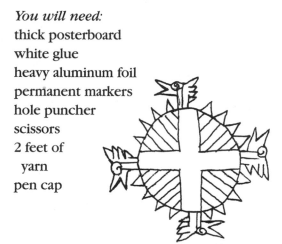

How to make a gorget:
1. Make a circle about 8 inches in diameter on a piece of posterboard. Round it off so it looks like the examples.
2. Copy your design on a separate piece of posterboard. You may need more than one piece of posterboard to make it thick.
3. Cut out your design and glue it to your circle. It should pop out.
4. Let the glue dry a long time, even overnight.
5. Lay a piece of foil on top of the gorget. Smooth it out and be careful not to rip the foil.
6. Using the pen cap, crease the foil around the edges of your design.

7. Color with permanent markers.

8. Punch two holes in the upper area and tie a piece of string through them, so it looks like a necklace.

OUR VISION FOR A BETTER TOMORROW

Writing this chapter about the Muscogee (Creek) Nation has helped us share this great heritage with you. Even though the Muscogee carry on many traditions from their past, they are like other Americans in many ways, too. They live in houses, wear regular clothes, and play soccer and kickball. If you were to talk to the members of the Fife family, your head would be full of neat ideas about them and their heritage.

The Fifes believe that going to school and getting a great education are very important. They have shown us that if you study hard, you can do great things for your community, like they have done for theirs. The Fifes have learned to follow their dreams, because they know dreams can come true.

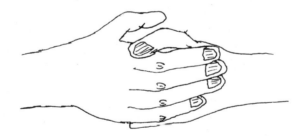

EXPLORING THE
ARAPAHO HERITAGE
WITH CAROLYN McLAUGHLIN

Reaching out with a helpful hand,
She teaches others to understand.
A proud Arapaho woman with a smile on her face
Working hard to make the world a better place.

Do you have something that you really believe in? We met a person who has a wonderful dream. She has been able to make her dream come true and help many people understand the beauty in different cultures. She wants people of all cultures to get along and understand each other.

CAROLYN McLAUGHLIN'S STORY

Carolyn McLaughlin remembers the first time she visited Arapahoe High School in Littleton, Colorado, and saw the school's logo or mascot—an Arapaho warrior. A logo is an art symbol for the school's team name, like the Denver Broncos or the Chicago Bulls. The Arapahoe High School logo was painted on the floor and looked

like a silly cartoon character. It didn't include any traditional Arapaho things like a headdress. Carolyn was offended to think that others might see an Arapaho warrior in this way. She thought to herself, "That doesn't look like an Arapaho warrior our people would be proud of."

This logo had been used for years and was an important part of the school. The school was proud of the name "Arapahoe Warriors," just as the Arapaho Nation has great respect for the Arapaho warriors. Even though the high school spelled its name with an "e" at the end, it was named after the Arapaho people.

Mrs. McLaughlin wanted to bring recognition and honor to her people and make the logo better. She worked with the school and they agreed to change their logo. Today, the logo looks like a real Arapaho warrior wearing a traditional headdress; it was drawn by an Arapaho artist named Wilbur Antelope. Mrs. McLaughlin helped to build a bridge of friendship between the school and her people so everyone could be proud.

September 17, 1993, was an important day in the history of Arapahoe High School and the Arapaho Nation. Many Arapaho Indian leaders stood beside Mrs. McLaughlin in front of the packed gym and looked at the crowd. The Great Plains Arapaho Eagle Drummers beat their elkskin drum and sang Arapaho songs. There was an awesome sharing of pride and respect when the drum began to play a friendship song and one by one the students joined in the dancing. "This is the first time in Colorado history that the Arapaho Nation has been recognized for its strength, honor, dignity, pride, and intelligence," said Mrs. McLaughlin.

The *Denver Post* headline read, "Warriors' logo changed in gesture of peace." The article told the story of how Carolyn McLaughlin, an Arapaho woman, helped Arapahoe High School, the community, and her nation reach out to each other in friendship.

The Arapaho Nation and Arapahoe High School have started an important relationship. The Arapaho Nation has shared a real

logo and the high school is going to return the gift by doing several things. The school promised to buy and display original Arapaho artifacts and to invite Arapaho artists and dancers to perform. The school will set up student exchanges between the Nation and the school and will give scholarships to students from the Arapaho Nation. The nation agreed to let Araphoe High School use the logo for school activities, but it must never be put on the floor because that would be disrespectful.

Everyone was happy about the new logo. Mrs. McLaughlin was excited to think that she had helped to change history for the high school and her people. Mrs. McLaughlin said, "May the Great Spirit guide those who cannot find a better way to remove barriers placed between us."

Now we would like to tell you the story of Carolyn McLaughlin's life. She was born on August 16, 1965, a warm afternoon, in Riverton, Wyoming. Her parents, Mr. and Mrs. Lawrence Miller, are both Native Americans. Her mother is Shoshone and her father is Arapaho and French. Carolyn has three older brothers and one older sister.

The family is very close and lives on the Wind River Reservation in western Wyoming at a place called Big Wind, near the Wind River Mountains. Not many people live around there. Carolyn knew everyone who lived nearby because most of them were her aunts, uncles, or cousins. Because Carolyn was lucky enough to live on a ranch, she got to have a paint horse named Pinto that she loved to ride. One year she decided to enter a horse competition and show her pretty, talented horse. After months of hard work with Pinto, she took him to the county fair. Pinto was named the Grand Champion. He and Carolyn won a ribbon, a trophy, a halter, and good prize money.

The Millers' ranch house looks just like one you might see in your neighborhood. They have a car, a television, and many of the things you have. Carolyn liked riding her bike over to her cousins' house to play. She liked hunting and fishing near the ranch. Her family lived far away from stores, so they usually planned a trip to town about once a week.

Carolyn's family has always been an important part of her life. Her father was a rancher and a judge and was highly respected in the community. He was called Chief Judge Lawrence Miller. He built the house they lived in, kept the ranch going, and helped many families with community problems and the law. He always believed in himself. Judge Miller worked very hard with children. He helped young people start a good life and stay away from violence. Carolyn said that her father was a stern man with a good, honest heart. His decisions made her notice how much he cared about people. She remembers him as a good leader who wouldn't back down from anything.

Nancy Miller, Carolyn's mother, is a strong woman who has taught her family about their heritage. She raised all of her children and is proud of them. She was a part-time teacher and now likes to work in her garden and run the ranch. Carolyn told us her mom is a great cook because she always uses fresh foods like vegetables, beef, and fish. She is also an artist and makes beautiful traditional items such as ribbon shirts and star-quilted blankets. She taught her children the importance of family and having respect for yourself and others.

Carolyn attended grade school on the Wind River Reservation. Arapaho Elementary School was just like any other school except that 95 percent of the kids were Native American. That means if there were 100 students, 95 were Native American and five were not. The school is very nice and has a swimming pool, a large gym, and a super track. It is kept very clean and each student has his or her own locker. There were about 250 students when Carolyn went there.

School subjects were about the same for Carolyn as they are for us today. One special thing they did in the eighth grade was take a class trip to celebrate their graduation from grade school. Carolyn still remembers when her class decided to go to Disneyland. Her dream of going there was going to finally come true! She couldn't wait to get out of school to run home to tell her Mom.

Then came the hard part. The class had to raise money so they could pay for the trip. They did lots of things like selling candy and cookies. They even ironed clothes!

Finally, all the money was raised and Carolyn, her 24 classmates, and two teachers boarded the bus. Off they went to California. Carolyn was amazed at how the land changed as they traveled to California. They left the mountains and plains behind. They drove through a desert. Carolyn loved looking at the unusual cacti. Then they started to see palm trees and land that had lots of plants.

It wasn't too long before the bus full of excited eighth-graders arrived in California. They stayed in a big hotel near Disneyland and did many wonderful things. The whole trip was lots of fun, but nothing was as great for Carolyn as going to Disneyland for the first time. It was the best place she had ever visited.

Her class came home and finished the eighth grade year and got ready to go to high school. Things changed when Carolyn went to high school. This was the first time she was around lots of kids who weren't

Native American. She had two groups of friends. One was mostly Indian, the other wasn't. Unfortunately, her two groups of friends did not get along very well. She didn't understand why they couldn't accept each others' differences.

Many of her Native American friends decided to quit school or transfer to another high school because they didn't like the attitude of this school. The school made some of her friends feel they weren't as good as the other kids just because they were different. It was as if Carolyn was living two separate lives, one in a white environment and the other in a Native American environment. It was hard to find a way to be accepted in a culture that felt so different from her own. It was like learning a new language.

Carolyn didn't feel good about some of the things that were happening in her school, but she was strong and stayed in school to graduate. Although high school was a tough time, she worked very hard to get good grades so that she could win a scholarship to college and learn how to help her people. She thought, "If I can go to college, I know I can learn to make the world a better place for Native Americans to live."

After she graduated from high school, Carolyn went to Central Wyoming College, a two-year college, because she couldn't afford to go away to a four-year university. The college was small, and once again she worked hard. After her first year in college, the Arapaho Nation gave her a scholarship so that she could attend Pikes Peak

College in Colorado Springs, Colorado. She was scared, but she left her home in Wyoming to attend school. All of a sudden, Carolyn's life was really different. There were people around her all the time and every place felt so crowded. Her family and friends seemed millions of miles away. Living in the city made her think about how much she wanted to go back home.

Carolyn remembers one of the most painful talks she ever had. It was with her hero, her father. Once when she was feeling very homesick at college, she called home for advice. She thought her dad would tell her that he missed her too and ask her to come home, but he didn't. He did tell her how much he loved her, but he also told her that she had to stay strong. He said that she needed to learn how the world works so she could bring that knowledge home and share it with others. Now Carolyn realizes how strong her father was and feels lucky that he encouraged her to stay and get her college degree.

Carolyn knew she wanted to help her people but she was not sure which classes to take. She had many decisions to make and felt confused. Finally, she decided to go for what she thought was "the American dream." She had heard that the American dream was to own a business, be the boss, and make lots of money.

Later on, Carolyn found her own dream. Just like some of her high school friends, Carolyn's college friends came from different backgrounds and did not always treat each other nicely. She did not know what to do about that, but she knew that hating other people was wrong. She wanted to help all groups of people understand one another. That's when she decided what her own dream was. It wasn't making money. It was to build a bridge between Native Americans and non-Natives. She wanted everyone to respect each other.

Carolyn started working to make her dream come true by studying business. She studied hard and got very good grades. Dr. Boissell, a white man, was one of her favorite teachers. He helped her with her vocabulary, encouraged her to stay in school, and even helped her find her first job in business. Carolyn thought her first job was neat. She was an office manager for a business that did screen printing on T-shirts and other clothing. She loved watching the artists put designs on the shirts. Her job was to keep track of how much time the employees worked so that they could be paid. She also kept track of the money, took orders from people wanting to buy shirts, and answered the phone. Carolyn feels grateful to Dr. Boissell for his encouragement and help with her first job. She said that without him she might not have her own business today.

Carolyn's last name wasn't always McLaughlin. She was born Carolyn Miller, but that changed because of a bike ride. One day she was riding her bike home from work when she met a man walking his dog. He was friendly and said, "Hello." Little did she know that a year and a half later, on July 7, 1986, she would be marrying that same man! His name is Athens McLaughlin. Mr. McLaughlin is part Span-

ish, Mayan Indian, French Canadian, and Irish. He is dedicated to keeping kids off drugs and safe from violence. Carolyn admires him because of his courage, strength, and honor. He has always been supportive of Carolyn's dream and encouraged her to be a businesswoman.

After Mrs. McLaughlin finished college, she worked in the business world to get more experience and learn how other businesses work. Then she started working to start her own business. It wasn't easy because she needed to learn many things and find some money to start it. After reading lots of books on law, she decided to get help from the Bureau of Indian Affairs (BIA), a government agency that is supposed to help Native Americans. There were many disappointments along the way, but Carolyn kept on going and refused to give up. At one point, the Small Business Administration wanted her to work for them as Indian Coordinator. Carolyn turned down this chance for a good job because she couldn't give up her dream of having her own business. She went to many banks for loans to start her business. Finally she got a small business loan after a year and a half of hard work, and she was able to buy what she needed to get started.

Then Mrs. McLaughlin took the big step: she opened her business, called Transitions Unlimited, which helps young people prepare for the future and become successful and happy. Transitions Unlimited holds two special events each year. One is American Indian Awareness Day; the other is the Youth Educational Encampment. Mrs. McLaughlin's programs find ways to teach young people about Native American culture and to develop leadership and social skills that will help them stay away from alcohol, drugs, and violence.

While we were writing this chapter, we were lucky enough to go to an American Indian Awareness Day that Mrs. McLaughlin's company put together at Arapahoe High School. Mrs. McLaughlin worked for months to raise money for the Awareness Day, getting everything organized and contacting all the people who were going to take part. The celebration

Ron Horn

Indian Awareness Day at Arapahoe High School

had interesting demonstrations and booths that sold all kinds of Indian artwork.

Mrs. McLaughlin had arranged for Billy Mills, a Native American who won a gold medal in the 1964 Olympics, to speak at the school assembly. He talked about how to motivate yourself, follow your dreams, and be successful. We also got to hear Mrs. McLaughlin speak to the high school students. We learned about the pride Arapahoe High School shares with the Arapaho Nation. We learned to appreciate each other and understand how we can be respectful of all cultures. Even adults enjoyed this special day. They found out they are never too old to learn this lesson, too.

Carolyn McLaughlin's Personal Statement

When you are a young person suddenly faced with responsibilities or peer pressure, you might not always make the right decisions for your life. Something to remember is that there will always be tomorrow.

It is important to learn from your mistakes and allow the hard lessons you learn in life to guide you to better yourself. As you get older, you will look back on your life and begin to be thankful for the many stepping stones and hard knocks you went through to get where you are today. As you grow in knowledge, physical appearance, or success, you must never forget who you are inside. A tiny voice is always with you inside, and that voice will let you know

Jeff Damas

Carolyn McLaughlin plays her guitar for the students

right from wrong. Be patient, wise, and strong because one day you will be faced with situations where you must make decisions for yourself, your families, schools, businesses, and communities.

THE FAMILY

In many Native American families, some of the members decide to stay on the reservation while others might decide to live someplace else. We would like you to know where the rest of Carolyn's family is and what they are doing today.

Benjamin Miller, Carolyn's brother, is the oldest in the family. He does a lot in his community and is the chairman of the Arapaho Elementary School Board. He worked with teachers and board members to design one of the best computer laboratories in the state of Wyoming. When he is not helping others, he is at home with his family or working on the cattle ranch and in the alfalfa fields. Benjamin also has a full-time job running heavy earth-moving equipment and

checking pressure gauges for large industrial plants. He has two daughters and two sons.

Robert Miller, Carolyn's second oldest brother, has a lot of experience in ranching. He works closely with other family members to run the ranch, plant crops and water them, brand cattle, and keep things working. He has six daughters and a brand-new grandson. In his free time, Robert likes to work with wood and make things out of willow branches like slingshots, arrows, and talking sticks.

Marilyn Monroe is Carolyn's only sister. Because she shares her name with a famous movie star, people always remember it and have fun with it. She likes that. Marilyn is a registered nurse and works in a small town near the Arapaho community. She likes her work because it is rewarding and challenging. Since she is a nurse, she always

Bud Miller (right) and friend build a tipi

remembers to be thankful for her good health. During her free time, Marilyn does Indian beadwork which she learned from her grandmother. She also spends time with her two sons and her daughter.

Buddy Miller, Carolyn's youngest brother, has always liked art. He has two Associate of Fine Arts degrees and his work has been shown in art galleries in Wyoming, Montana, Colorado, New Mexico, and Arizona. Buddy has two daughters. He likes to be outside and has been a saddle bronc horse rider and a bull rider in many rodeos. He is also a drummer and singer in many pow-wows. Buddy teaches art at the Arapaho Elementary School in Wyoming.

THE ARAPAHO NATION

The Arapaho people have lived on this continent for hundreds of years. They hunted buffalo on the Great Plains. The meat and hides from the buffalo provided them with food, clothing, and shelter. In the 1700s the Arapaho got to know the white people and became smart traders. The name Arapaho may have come from the Indian word *tirapihu*, or trader. Other people believe the name came from the Crow word *alappaho*, which means "people with many tattoos." Many Arapaho men had three small circles drawn across their chests, while the women had one circle on their foreheads.

The Arapaho lived in tipis made from small poles covered with 15 to 20 buffalo hides sewn together. The

inside was lined and painted with pictures of the father's great deeds. Many families made camp together during the spring buffalo hunt, in a peaceful valley. The tipis were put in a big circle, so that the center area could be used for ceremonies. During the fall, the people broke up into smaller groups and moved back to their homes in the forests.

After the Europeans came to America, Arapaho life changed because there weren't enough buffalo anymore. It became harder to hunt for buffalo, and white settlers and the Arapaho started fighting a lot.

As more and more settlers moved west, the Arapaho people were split into two large groups. The Southern Arapaho moved south. They weren't given a reservation and now many of them live in Oklahoma. The

ARAPAHO NATION

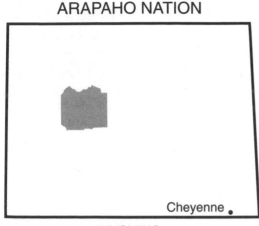

WYOMING

Northern Arapaho moved north to the Wind River Reservation in Wyoming.

The Wind River Reservation has about 3,500 square miles and is surrounded by mountains and national forests. The Arapaho and Shoshone Nations share the reservation. Most of the people live in the valleys and on the plains. Riverton is the only city on the reservation. Fort Washakie, named after a Shoshone leader, is the headquarters for the Arapaho and Shoshone tribal governments.

The Arapaho tribal government doesn't have a chief. It is run by a committee of Arapaho who are elected by tribal members. The committee is called the General Council. They deal with important issues like water, oil, gas, and taxes. The General Council works with Congress, federal agencies, governors, and even the president of the United States. This Council represents the Arapaho people and deals with the U.S. government just like any other nation. The Council works hard to make life as good as possible for the Arapaho today.

CUSTOMS AND TRADITIONS

Different families practice their heritage in different ways. Mrs. McLaughlin's family took a very active part in the community and went to many powwows. A powwow is a Native American celebration where songs and dances are shared. The family also sews traditional clothing and makes traditional works of art like those of their tribal ancestors.

The customs of song and dance have special meaning to the Arapaho people and are important parts of Carolyn McLaughlin's life. She sang and played some traditional songs for us. She taught us how to sing a neat song called "Star Walker" using the guitar. The song puts Indian and modern music together. It was made famous by Buffy St. Marie. You can buy her tape, *Coincidence and Likely Stories*, in music stores.

We learned to keep the beat to Native American music with a bell on a string. Then Mrs. McLaughlin showed us how to do a circle dance and play our bells to keep the beat as we danced. Many Native Americans dance at powwows and other occasions.

Sometimes at large powwows, many groups of Native Americans dance together. Each dancer designs his or her own regalia, which is the special clothing worn for a powwow. Their regalia shows some of the traditions in their nation. Mrs. McLaughlin told us that it is considered rude to use the word "costume" when talking about a person's regalia.

People can dance in competitions or just dance together. Each dance has special steps. Fancy Dance is a favorite dance for the young people. This dance has lots of high steps and quick turns and is pretty fancy. The Jingle Dance is also popular. When you do this dance, you don't move around very much, and you take slow turns. Traditional Dance is another style of dancing done by many older people.

Arapaho Elementary School on the reservation has special teachers who come in and teach the children about their culture. One of these teachers is Mrs. Mary Ann Whiteman. She is Mrs. McLaughlin's aunt.

When she was younger, she taught her own children about their heritage. Today she is an elder and teaches some of us about our heritage. She teaches Arapaho values such as having respect for yourself, your elders, and everything around you. She shares some stories from the past. Some stories are about history, while others teach a lesson. Sometimes she teaches Arapaho words.

During culture class, Mrs. Whiteman talks about traditions from the past—like how tipis were made. The hide or skin was taken off the buffalo and stretched over tree branches. The hair was scraped off the hide with bones. Then the women would rub some of the buffalo's brain on the hide to

Transitions Unlimited

Mary Ann Whiteman (center, seated) at youth camp

HISTORY TIMELINE

1700s The Arapaho lived on the Great Plains and hunted the large herds of buffalo that roamed the plains from the Rocky Mountains to the Missouri River. They met white settlers and began trading with them.

1803 The United States government bought a large piece of land from France. It was called the Louisiana Purchase. It included land that the Arapaho had lived on for hundreds of years.

1840 White settlers started coming west on the Oregon Trail through what is now Wyoming.

1848 Gold was discovered in California, so many more settlers came west.

1850s As more and more settlers came west, the Arapaho tribe was split into two parts, northern and southern. By 1855 the two groups were separate from each other.

1851 The Treaty of Fort Laramie was signed. It was the first treaty between the U.S. government and several Native American nations, including the Arapaho. This treaty said that many Plains Indians had to live in certain areas. The Arapaho and Cheyenne were given a reservation near the upper Arkansas River in an area that is now Colorado.

1861 The U.S. government made a treaty with the Arapaho and Cheyenne. It said that all Arapaho and Cheyenne had to live on the reservations and the government would protect them and help them keep that land for their homes.

1864-68 The Sand Creek Massacre happened after the U.S. government promised to keep the Arapaho and Cheyenne safe and the Indians gave up their weapons. Then Reverend General Chivington attacked and killed many Indians.

1865-68 Many treaties were signed between the U.S. government and the Arapaho. The government forced tribes to give up their tribal lands and move. The Arapaho had to let the railroad, wagon trains, and roads go through their land, and they had to send all children between the ages of 6 and 16 to school. Indian people had to change the way they had always lived because they could no longer travel around the Great Plains and hunt.

1870s After hard times in the early 1870s, the northern Arapaho worked as scouts for the U.S. Army and became more friendly with the Army.

1877 Three Northern Arapaho leaders, Black Coal, Sharp Nose, and Friday, went to Washington, D.C., to meet with President Rutherford B. Hayes. They got permission to settle on the Shoshone reservation in Wyoming.

1884 Black Coal, a leader of the Arapaho, allowed the Catholics to use some land to set up St. Stephen's Mission.

1887 The U.S. Congress passed the General Allotment Act and once again took land away from Native Americans. The reservation land that was owned by the tribe was split up into little parts, called allotments, which were given to each tribal member. Then all of their leftover land was sold to white settlers. In the 1890s the settlers moved onto their allotments on the reservation.

1904 In the 1904 Agreement, the U.S. government took away two-thirds of the northern Arapaho and Shoshone land.

1910 Arapaho leaders sold land to the Episcopal Church and the Episcopalians started St. Michael's Mission. The small town of Arapaho grew up around this church.

1924 All Native Americans became citizens of the United States when the U.S. government passed the Snyder Act.

1961 The northern and southern Arapaho received a settlement from the government because the government had broken so many treaties with them.

1993 The Arapaho Nation and Arapahoe High School in Colorado started working together to encourage respect.

soften it. This was called brain tanning. The brain would soak into the hide and help make it strong.

Even today you will see tipis on the reservation in the summer. Families put up their tipis so they can enjoy the cool fresh air outside or just to check them and make sure they are in good shape. Today, tipis are made out a material called canvas instead of buffalo hide. Some tipis are about 12 feet high and hold about 20 people. There are also big tipis that are about 50 feet high and hold about 100 people.

We would like you to know good tipi manners. Before you go into a tipi, you scratch on the door instead of knocking. It is still a custom to keep everything really neat inside a tipi. This was done in the past so the family could move at a moment's notice. Today it is done to carry on the custom from the past and to learn to be neat.

There are many ceremonies held during the summer on the reservation. We are going to show our respect for the Arapaho by not putting details about special ceremonies in this book. Mrs. McLaughlin said that spiritual traditions have been passed down from generation to generation. She believes that these are sacred and should only be shared with members of the tribe. It would be disrespectful to the Arapaho people if we talked about their sacred events. Being respectful is important to us because one of the reasons we are writing this book is to learn and teach respect for all cultures.

STORIES AND LEGENDS

Many cultures, including the Arapaho, have stories that have been told for many generations. We heard many Arapaho stories and legends. A legend is a tale that is passed on from generation to generation by tradition. Many people think of it as telling about history, even though its truth cannot be checked. If you read carefully, you might be able to understand the lessons that are explained in these stories. Here is the legend of "The Talking Stick" that was retold for us by an Arapaho elder. This story is special to Carolyn McLaughlin because her brother carves talking sticks.

The Talking Stick

Once there was a young and handsome Arapaho warrior. The warrior's grandfather named him Stops the Enemy. His grandfather taught him how important it was to share knowledge and stories. Stops the Enemy grew up to be a great hunter and quite a fast runner. Although he had many talents, he was pretty quiet unless he was with the Arapaho children. He saw that the children learned quickly and respected what he said.

Stops the Enemy always carried a special stick. His grandfather had given him the stick. It was a piece of driftwood that had been carved by the water. Stops the Enemy used the stick when he was talking to children. He explained that only the person who was holding the stick could talk. Then he had the children sit in a circle. The

child who was holding the stick told a story. When the story was done, that child passed the stick around the circle to give someone else a turn to tell a story.

Sometimes the children were shy and couldn't think of a story, so Stops the Enemy tied pretty beads, feathers, and stones to the stick. This gave them something to talk about. When the children held the beautifully decorated stick, they got ideas for stories about nature, such as the uses of stones, high-flying birds, or the beautiful colors on the earth.

The children always listened carefully to Stops the Enemy so that they could learn from him when they had their talking circles. Stops the Enemy taught them it was important for elders to share their stories with children and for children to share their stories with their elders. This was a great way to share, have fun, and learn.

The talking stick teaches people to take turns and listen to others. Do you have problems with listening or being interrupted? Maybe your class or family needs to make a talking stick!

Getting a Traditional Name

Do you know how your mom and dad came up with your name? Here is a legend that explains how the Arapaho get their Indian names.

A long time ago, when women had babies, the mothers did not know what to name them. So they would take their babies to the wise man. One day a woman had a baby and took it to the wise man for a name. The wise man named him Spirit of the Eagles. A year later the child's mom took him to the wise man for a new name. The wise man named him Man of the Moon.

Ten years later the child's mom took him back to the wise man and said, "Wise man, can you give my child a new name?" So the wise man named him Running Warrior. The next day, Running Warrior's family had a feast to celebrate all his names.

Later, when Running Warrior was an old man, a woman in his tribe had a baby and did not know what to name him. Running Warrior went over to her house and asked if he could give his name to the baby.

The woman asked, "What is your name?"

Running Warrior replied, "Running Warrior." The woman said that it would be a perfect name for her baby. Running Warrior, the wise man, gave the child his name, and a year later the wise old man died. The legend says that Arapaho people have named their children in this way ever since then. That is how all their names came to be. Names are a gift to remember other great people who had the same name.

FOOD AND FUN

We will show you how to make some delicious food and enjoy some Arapaho crafts and games in this section.

No-Bake Cookies

We had a lot of fun spending time with Mrs. McLaughlin. Like us, she enjoys eating many different kinds of food. We decided to include her favorite recipe, which happens not to be Native American. She taught us how to make No-Bake Cookies and we couldn't wait to taste them. You might want to wear an apron when you make them, because things can get a little messy!

You will need:
2 cups white sugar
½ cup milk
½ stick margarine
¼ cup cocoa
1 teaspoon vanilla
3 cups instant oatmeal

How to make the cookies:
1. Mix the first four ingredients into a saucepan together.
2. Cook them on the stove until they boil, then turn off the heat and put the pan on a hotpad.
3. Add the vanilla and stir it in.
4. Then stir in the oatmeal.
5. Put enough cookie dough on a teaspoon to fill up the spoon. Then drop the dough onto waxed paper.

6. Let the dough cool for about an hour until the cookies are hardened and ready to eat.

We hope you enjoy these sweet, chocolatey cookies as much as we did!

Dried Beef Jerky

Another recipe Mrs. McLaughlin likes is dried beef jerky. She has made this recipe using venison (deer meat) instead of beef.

You will need:

3 pounds beef brisket
1 teaspoon garlic powder
1 tablespoon ground pepper
1 tablespoon salt
½ cup Worcestershire sauce
⅓ cup soy sauce

How to make the jerky:

1. On a cutting board, cut the meat into thin, ¼- to ⅛-inch strips. Be sure to cut across the grain in the meat. You should ask one of your parents or an older person to do this for you.

2. Soak the meat strips in a glass or plastic container with the rest of the ingredients for at least 24 hours. (Do not use a metal pan because it will make the meat taste bad.) Make sure the strips lay flat and the sauce covers the meat. If it doesn't, turn the meat over after about 12 hours.

3. Then put the meat strips in a single layer on a cooking rack resting on a baking sheet. Bake the meat in a 140- to 170-degree oven for 12 hours, or until it's dry and bendable. Be sure not to leave the meat in the oven too long or it will overbake and be too hard to eat.

Other ways to use beef jerky:

1. Cook in water until tender. Then chop in a blender and add the little pieces to cornmeal gravy.

2. Roast and eat with chile and tortillas.

3. Use in tamales.

4. Make jerky hash.

5. Add to any kind of stew.

6. Boil small pieces in water, then add dumplings.

7. Try jerky with chile for breakfast.

8. Fry small pieces of jerky in a little shortening. Add 2 cups of water and heat until it boils. Crack an egg (throw the shell away!) and put into the pan with the jerky. Turn off the heat, put a lid on the pan, and let it sit until the egg white is hard.

9. Broil jerky until crisp. Keep an eye on it, because it burns fast!

Making Moccasins

Mrs. McLaughlin showed us beautiful moccasins made by her grandmother. They had lots of details and colorful beadwork that has special meaning to the Arapaho. She told us how special these moccasins were to her and how she would never give them up for anything. We thought how proud she must be to have this beautiful keepsake to remember her grandmother by since she has passed away. Her grandmother and sister taught Carolyn how to make moccasins and now she teaches other people, like us, how to make them.

You will need:
brown paper grocery bag
scissors
chalk, pencil, or marker
leather or sturdy fabric
string
needle
markers or beads to decorate with

How to make moccasins:
1. Cut the brown paper bag open so that it is a flat piece.
2. Step on the paper and use chalk to trace around your foot. Remember to stand with

all your weight on the paper so your moccasin will fit when you walk. Write "right" or "left" on your footprint so you know which foot each one fits.

3. Trace your other foot. You need to do both feet because they are a little different in size.

4. Cut a large rectangle of brown paper to lay on the top of your foot. Make a small slit about 3 or 4 inches long in one end for your ankle to fit in.

5. Hold the paper around your foot and use the chalk to trace about half an inch away from your foot so that you will have room to sew the material.

6. Plan the decorations for your moccasins by drawing designs on the outside of the pattern pieces.

7. Trace every piece you have cut out onto cloth or leather, and cut them out again.

8. Decorate the top piece of your moccasin with beads, markers, or fabric paint.

9. Use the needle and thread to sew the top part of your moccasin to the sole. Keep trying on your moccasins after you sew every couple of inches to make sure they will fit.

10. You are finally finished. Enjoy them, you earned it!

Pa-Tol Game

Pa-tol is a lot like the games Sorry and Trouble that many kids play. But it is a little different because it is played on the ground with rocks. Here is how you play Pa-tol.

First you need to find 40 stones that are the size of your fist and place them in a cir-

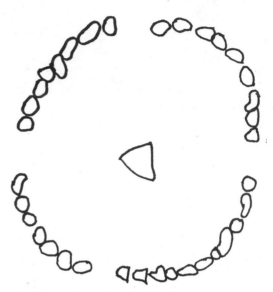

cle that is four feet around. Put openings between the stones at the north, south, east, and west parts of the circle. These openings are called rivers. Put a large rock in the middle of the circle.

Now you need to make the die. It's like a regular die except it is larger and made out of rock, not plastic. Find a squarish rock and paint dots on it to stand for the numbers.

Finally, find a stone for your game piece. Two to four people play this game, and each player needs a game piece.

Now you're ready to play Pa-tol! First, all the players put their stone game piece on a different river. Throw the die when it's your turn, then move your piece however many spaces you rolled on the die. If you land on another player's piece, you need to go back to your river and wait for your next turn.

The first person to get around the circle and back to their river with the exact number wins. If you don't land exactly on your river, you need to keep going around until you do. Have fun!

Hand Game

There are several Native American hand games and here is one of them. This game does not have a special name. Native Americans played hand games to improve their observation skills. This game is usually played with two teams of two players each. The teams sit across from each other. One team is called the "lookers," the other team is the "doers."

The doer team starts with two small sticks about two inches long. This team passes the sticks to each other, hiding them in their hands and trying to trick the other team by not letting them see who has the sticks. Meanwhile, the second team is trying to keep track of where the sticks are.

When someone says, "Stop!" the doer team puts out their closed hands. One person on the looker team points with their right hand to the person they think has the sticks. If they think the player on the left has the sticks, they point with their index finger. If they think the player on the right has the sticks, they point with their pinkie. If they are correct, they win a point. Then it is their turn to pass the sticks while the other team watches.

OUR VISION FOR A BETTER TOMORROW

Just as Mrs. McLaughlin has a vision for a better future, so do we, the authors of this chapter. Here are some things we would like to share with you.

Dear Readers,

We would like to talk about what we are really like as Native Americans on the Wind River Reservation.

For one thing, our skin is not red. It is kind of brown. Some Native Americans like to call it whitish. People in cities sometimes think that Native Americans still wear traditional clothes like buckskins, beaded moccasins, and feather headdresses, but we don't. We dress just like other people. Mostly we wear blue jeans, T-shirts, sweatshirts, sneakers, and jackets. But we do wear traditional clothes for powwows and other ceremonies.

We live in houses, not tipis. Our houses are like many other houses. They have bedrooms, kitchens, bathrooms, and living rooms. Tipis are used for special occasions. In the summertime, they can be seen across the reservation.

We do not have to hunt for food because we buy it at a regular store. We hunt for deer, antelope, and elk only during hunting season.

Many Native Americans are successful and find good jobs. The Arapaho Tribal Council hires people and encourages them to stay in school and get an education because there aren't many good jobs on the reservation. Some of the people that live here try to get better jobs, but it is hard because they have to leave their family and friends behind.

We speak the same language as everybody else, English. But we speak Arapaho, too. We can write the alphabet in Arapaho and say Arapaho words.

Some city people think we travel on horses, but we don't. We get around by cars, trucks, and bikes.

So, today our lives are just like everyone else's. We are glad you have been interested in our heritage. We hope you will continue to learn more. We hope you have been able to understand our traditions—both old and new.

EXPLORING THE NAVAJO HERITAGE WITH JUDGE ALLEN SLOAN

Every day Judge Sloan lends a hand,
To help our people across our land,
He's reached his goals along the way,
That's what makes him such a strong judge today.

On June 7, 1989, in Window Rock, Arizona, Allen Sloan stood proud and tall as he took the oath of office. He was only 30 years old and the youngest man ever to be sworn in as judge for the Navajo Nation. Since that time, Judge Sloan has been a role model for the Navajo Nation and for the children who look up to him. Here is his story.

JUDGE ALLEN SLOAN'S STORY

Some people go to work every day just to earn a paycheck, even if it's to do something they don't like to do. Many people are grateful just for a job that pays. But Judge Sloan loves his job and gets a good income, too. His job as a judge means he needs to know the Navajo language, Navajo traditions, and the way the Navajo government and laws work.

Allen Sloan has been a judge for six years. He works about ten hours a day and spends most of that time in his chambers. A judge's chambers are his offices near the courtroom. Judge Sloan uses his chambers for meeting with people and for reading and writing his decisions after studying cases very, very carefully. During trials in the courtroom, he sits on a platform called a bench and pounds a gavel to call the court to order. He wears a black robe and has to keep a straight face so no one can accuse him of taking sides. There are rules for visitors in court, too. People can't chew gum, wear hats, or move around much, because it breaks the judge's concentration.

Judge Sloan thinks of himself as a traditional Navajo. He is proud when he looks

John Cozzens

The Window Rock, across the street from Navajo headquarters

back on his life. His childhood name was Askie Lichosce, meaning "fair-haired boy." Navajo children are given names that identify them by their looks, or by something important that happened to them. Later, secret Navajo names are given by a medicine man during a special ceremony. Allen Sloan has a secret Navajo name, but he couldn't share it with us, or it wouldn't be a secret anymore!

Allen Sloan was raised by his grandparents and by his aunt and uncle. He grew up near Tuba City, Arizona, in an area called Coal Mine Mesa. It was always hot and dry, and the closest store was three miles from home. In the past, many Navajo children went to boarding schools, arranged by the Bureau of Indian Affairs. Allen went

to his first boarding school in Tuba City. He remembers having to stay until Christmas before he got to go home for a visit. He told us they were all kind of scared at first, but as time went on, he and the other Navajo kids got used to it. They ate, slept, and went to school in the same school buildings. After the Tuba City school, Allen was sent to another boarding school in Richford, Utah, a high school almost 400 miles from his home.

When Allen was a kid, he wanted to be a teacher. His favorite preschool teacher had been Mr. Johnson. One day Allen and his classmates were just plain sad. Mr. Johnson tried everything to cheer them up. Nothing worked. Then, all of a sudden, he reached into his mouth and pulled out all his top teeth! The class was amazed and shocked. Mr. Johnson said, "I bet you kids can't do that." All the kids tried, but they couldn't figure how he did it. For many nights afterward, Allen tried to get his own teeth out, but they wouldn't budge. When he got older, Allen found out about false teeth. He laughs today when he remembers how Mr. Johnson tricked them into believing he was a magician. When Judge Sloan talked with us, we could see how much he was like his favorite teacher, because he loves to show his funny side, too!

Summer vacations were always fun for Allen, but there was a lot of work to do, too. Sometimes he had to herd the sheep away from the house. When he did this, Allen was with the sheep from sunrise to sunset. The food his Grandma would fix—cheese, thick tortillas called *na'neeskadi'*,

a boat out of some tree bark, a small stick, and a green leaf by poking the stick through the piece of bark and attaching the green leaf to it. He would take his boat to the animals' water tank or a small pond and pretend it was a big boat on a big lake.

Often Allen would wander over to his cousin Norman's house. Allen and his cousin were the same age and lived across the valley from each other. They grew up together and were the best of friends. Norman was given the nickname Bunno from his last name, which was Bedonie. The boys would spend their time swimming, climbing rocks on the mesa, or just messing around all day. Allen and Bunno also made toy trucks. They would find a piece of wood and carve it until it looked like a truck. They pounded a nail in

and a small bottle of water—had to last him until dinner time. He kept all of this in a pouch that hung from straps at his side. He told us how the sheep always seemed hungry. They weren't lucky enough to have a good hot meal waiting for them in the evening like he did.

The Sloans had several horses for riding and pulling the family wagon. Sometimes, when the Sloans didn't have store-bought bridles, they used rope. If there wasn't any rope around, Allen used parts of a yucca plant to make ropes. The rope went around the horse's nose and tied under the horse's jaw for a set of reins.

Allen's family didn't have a television, so the kids spent a lot of time finding ways to entertain themselves. Sometimes they swam in the water tank where the animals drank. Sometimes they made their own toys. Allen remembers making

the front of the truck and attached a string to it, so that they could pull it around. "We played with those trucks for hours," Judge Sloan told us.

Allen remembers buying soda pop at the Coal Mine Trading Post. It was a general store that sold some groceries, clothing, and soda pop. When you bought pop in a can, the can was made out of tin, and you used a can opener or knife to open it. Sometimes the kids had to share one big bottle.

But it wasn't always fun for Allen and his friends. One day, when Allen was in fourth grade, he and a classmate went over to the school house and ended up pulling a girl's hair. The chase was on. Allen ran into a science room where a model of a Tyrannosaurus rex, a very large dinosaur, hung from the ceiling. The boys bumped the dinosaur and it came crashing down around them. The principal was so upset he called Allen's aunt and uncle and the parents of Allen's friend. It was decided the two were "out of control." So to teach the boys a lesson, the judge, who happened to

A Navajo reservation trading post

be Allen's uncle, sent them to jail. They had to stay only a couple of hours, but it was a very embarrassing experience for both of them. It kept them out of trouble for quite a while.

This was not the only hard time in Allen's life. We were thankful he decided to tell us this next story, and we will never forget how we felt when we heard it. Judge Sloan told us he wanted to share an important lesson he had learned in his life. We are telling it to you, so you can understand why it meant so much to us. Although these are not the Judge's exact words, we have decided to tell the story in the first person so you can hear it just like we did.

"More than ten years ago, when I was in my twenties, I had a Toyota pickup with a sunroof. I was very proud of that truck and took great care of it. But I was young and foolish and did some things I'm not very proud of. One night a friend and I took my truck to Tuba City. We were drinking. Very late that night, when we were coming back to Window Rock, my friend who was driving fell asleep. The truck flipped off the road, the sunroof broke, and I fell out of the truck. All of a sudden, I found myself sliding under the truck. My finger and leg got caught between the ground and the hood of the truck. When the truck skidded to a stop, my leg hurt bad and my little finger was gone. Because it was late at night, it was some time before someone found us and took us to the hospital.

"This accident made me realize I had to change something in my life. My truck was

John Cozzens

Judge Sloan shares his story with the student authors

ruined, and I knew I had nearly lost my life. That day, I decided I would never drink alcohol again.

"Today, I look at my hand, and I remember the promise I made to myself. When I was teaching my children to count on my fingers, I could count only to nine. But that's okay, because I told them about the time I learned a lesson that changed my life for the better. I hope you will learn from my experience, too."

When Judge Sloan was done sharing his story, you could have heard a pin drop in the room. We were all thinking about how brave he was to come and share with us, and we thank him for sharing from his heart. Judge Sloan taught us that life is not always easy. We hope that the kids who read his story will react like we did and stop and think. He made his dreams come true by remembering his promise and working very hard.

Judge Sloan's daughter Nina, who helped write this chapter, told us she wanted everyone to remember never to get into a car with someone who has been drinking.

Some people lose more than their pinky; they lose their life.

THE FAMILY

Judge Sloan is married to Beverly and they have three children. Anthony is seven, Noreen is eleven, and Nina is twelve. Mrs. Sloan works as an accountant. She likes reading about Navajo culture and learning about how Navajo ceremonies came to be. Both Judge and Mrs. Sloan love their family very much and want their children to know about modern-day life and to learn more about their Navajo culture and history. The family spends a lot of time together. If Mrs. Sloan is at work or going to school to finish her business degree, then Judge Sloan does the cooking. When the kids have homework, both mom and dad are willing to help, but they never give them the answers.

The Sloan family has lots of hobbies. Mrs. Sloan enjoys traveling, reading books, and eating Chinese food. Judge Sloan's hobbies are cooking, reading, and playing basketball and volleyball. He uses his lunchtime every day to jog and get relaxed, so he can think about the cases he's working on. His daughter Nina likes to read, swim, and ride horses. In the summer, she goes to camp to learn more about horseback riding. The camp has rodeos, barrel racing, pack trips on horses, and lots of other neat things. Nina's sister Noreen likes playing basketball, spending time with her Barbie dolls, and watching *Nickelodeon* on TV.

Their brother Anthony likes to play marbles and basketball and ride bikes with his best friend.

The whole family loves to go on trips together and sing songs as they drive along in the truck. This is when the children get to hear their mom and dad tell stories about when they were young. When the Sloans travel to faraway places like other states, they always have a great time together swimming, or shopping, or going out to dinner. Every year, the Sloan family gets together with relatives for a week of camping. Getting together is the main goal, but they like to fish, hike, and pick flowers, too. We saw some neat hats they made from plants they found.

THE NAVAJO NATION

The Navajo people lived in the deserts and mountains for hundreds of years. Today, the borders of Arizona, New Mexico, Utah, and Colorado cut through the traditional Navajo land between the four sacred mountains. The Navajo Nation is about the same size as West Virginia.

The Navajo learned their way of life from the Holy People. Their ancestors passed on the Navajo Way of living and growing crops with very little water in the dry, hot Southwest. They grew corn, squash, and melons. Corn was their most important

Leslie Nelson

A customer makes a purchase at the Navajo Arts and Crafts Store

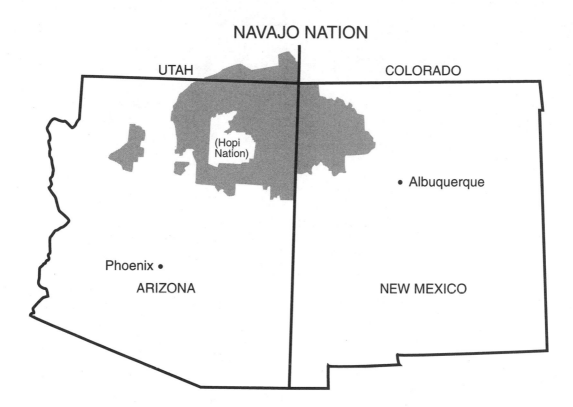

NAVAJO NATION

UTAH

COLORADO

(Hopi Nation)

• Albuquerque

Phoenix •

ARIZONA

NEW MEXICO

crop, and Navajo women knew many different ways to cook with it. Because the Navajo owned a lot of sheep, they always had wool for yarn to make rugs and blankets. Sheep were so valuable, they were given as gifts to people who had taken part in Navajo ceremonies.

Navajo families used to live in forkstick hogans made of poles, dirt, and branches or in circle-shape hogans made of logs that were filled in with dirt. As a sign of respect for the rising sun, hogans had doorways that always faced east.

In the past, the Navajo lived together with different families in groups called clans. Clans lived in different areas across the land. Today, clan members identify themselves by the area where their clan used to live. Instead of one chief for all the Navajo, each clan had a headman who watched over his group. After a man and woman were married, they moved into a hogan next to the woman's mother. Navajo women were very powerful and respected in their families, because they owned the sheep. It was the grandmother who taught the Navajo beliefs and values to her family.

Navajo customs helped the children learn how to live. When Navajo children were about five years old, they got their own lambs. Taking care of the lambs taught them how to work hard and be responsible. Girls learned from their mothers how to spin wool and make blankets. Boys

HISTORY TIMELINE

The beginning of Navajo history does not start with an exact date.

1500s The Navajo were living in the Southwest.

1848 The Mexican War ended. Mexico and the United States signed the Treaty of Guadalupe-Hidalgo. The U.S. claimed the land that the Navajo were already living on.

1849 U.S. troops killed Narbona, the Navajo leader. This started a fight between the U.S. and the Navajo.

1850 The U.S. Army built Fort Defiance in the middle of Navajo land.

1863 Navajo surrendered to U.S. troops and were forced to leave their homeland. They began the 250-mile walk to the Bosque Redondo Reservation in New Mexico, where they were imprisoned for four years. Many Navajo died during this hard time.

1868 In June, the Navajo were allowed to return to a small part of their homeland which had been made into a reservation.

1882 The United States government set up the Court of Indian Offenses, run by the Bureau of Indian Affairs. This was the beginning of the first Navajo courts.

1890 Navajo silversmiths started using turquoise in their jewelry.

1921 Oil was discovered on the Navajo reservation. Oil companies wanted the right to drill on Navajo land.

1923 The first meeting of the Navajo Tribal Council was held.

1932 The U.S. government and the Navajo Nation started working to stop soil erosion on reservation land.

1941 The U.S. entered World War II. Navajo men and women volunteered to fight for the U.S. Many Navajo worked as code talkers. They used the Navajo language as a secret code against the enemy.

1950 Laws were passed to help raise money to improve reservation schools.

1958 The Navajo Nation took control of the Court of Indian Offenses and tribal courts were formed.

1965 Office of Navajo Economic Opportunity was started.

1969 The Navajo Nation became the official name of the Navajo people and their reservation.

1989 Allen Sloan became the youngest Navajo judge in the history of the Nation.

learned how to herd sheep and how to track and hunt animals. Some were taught how to perform ceremonies.

Even a long time ago, the Holy People taught the Navajo to respect life and to keep a balance between the earth and man. Sickness and evil were signs that the normal balance had been upset. When this happened, the singer performed a ceremony to help the balance get back to normal.

Many Native Americans aren't as lucky as the Navajo who still live on the same land as their ancestors. The Navajo are one of the biggest tribes in the U.S. The Navajo Nation is proud of their museum and cultural arts center. Many Navajo still speak their traditional language and carry on many of the traditions from their past. People from all over the world come to see the beautiful Navajo reservation. Many want to buy their colorful blankets, rugs, and silver jewelry. The Navajo are world-famous for their rugs and turquoise jewelry. The Navajo Nation is working very hard to keep their people together in their homeland.

CUSTOMS AND TRADITIONS

The Navajo call themselves Dine, which means "the people." Navajo land is still called Dine'tah, which means "within the land of the people." Navajo is a Spanish word.

Most people use the directions north, south, east, and west to find things, but the Navajo are more serious about the four directions. The number four is very important in the Navajo way of life. There are usually four verses in the Navajo ceremonial songs used in healing, and there are four sacred mountains. All four directions have different meanings in Navajo.

The four sacred mountains that surround the Navajo reservation have special meanings, too. In the east you can see Blanca Peak. It is also called Dawn or White Shell Mountain. Flagstaff Mountain, called San Francisco Peak, rises in the west and stands for knowledge. It is also known as Abalone Shell Mountain. North stands for happiness, and in the north, one can see Mount Hesperus. Mount Taylor, also known as Blue Bead and Turquoise Mountain, is in the south.

The four mountains are important to the Navajo, because they help heal their minds and bodies and remind them that the four directions were given to them by the Holy People. Navajos don't go to the mountains to play or fool around, because they are considered very sacred. They don't spit or stomp on the mountains, because this would be disrespectful.

Clans

Judge Sloan has a clan. This is a large group of people who are related by ancestor or bloodline. Every Navajo person belongs to a clan. Clans are important to Judge Sloan and the Navajo because of the special relationship between its members. When you meet a new person in your clan for the first time, you take care of the new person just like you would a brother or sister, because your clan is the same. Children belong to their mother's clan. Clan members cannot marry one another.

Traditional Objects

Cradleboards are part of the Navajo past and are still used today for carrying babies. Just like all things in the Navajo way of life, the parts of a Navajo cradleboard stand for male and female. The two backboards show Mother Earth on the right, painted red, and Father Sky, on the left, painted blue, and remind the Navajo of where they come from. The strings that tie the baby in stand for lightning and the rain that brings life. The rainbow curved over the baby's head is a symbol of protection. Short rainbows on the back of the cradleboard tie the two boards together and protect the baby. Cradleboards are still very respected by the Navajo people.

Leslie Nelson

A Navajo reservation hogan

Hogans

Today, most Navajo live in regular houses but go to Navajo ceremonies in hogans. In the past, almost all Navajo lived in hogans. The Navajo hogan was the main center of life. There are female and male hogans. The female hogan is round and looks like a ball that has been cut in half. It is the place to eat, sleep, and cook. The male hogan, shaped like a cone with a circular inside area, is used for traditional ceremonies.

The door on a hogan faces east where the sun comes up. Navajo elders taught their people not to sleep when the sun comes up. If a sunbeam shines on you, the good spirits will think you are lazy and wonder if they want to help lazy people. So early in the morning before the sun came up, the Navajo would run to the east as far as they could. Running kept them from being lazy, and it kept them in good health, too.

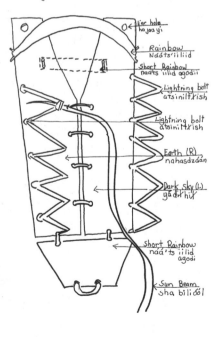

Navajo Cradleboard

Tribal Fair

A Navajo Tribal Fair happens during the second weekend in September in Window Rock, Arizona, the capital of the Navajo Nation. It is the largest Indian fair in North America. About ninety thousand people pay admission to get into the fair every fall. Rodeos, powwows, carnivals, concerts, song and dance contests, the Miss Navajo Pageant, and the parade are some of the many different events at the fair. The biggest attraction of all is the parade. The booths at the fair are really neat, too. Many of them are run by tribal members wearing traditional Navajo clothing.

The fair is a special gathering place for Navajo and others. It is a good place to see old friends and to make new ones. Long-lost relatives often come back for the fair. People of different cultures come and learn more about the Navajo and enjoy their traditional arts and great food. There is something for everyone, young and old.

STORIES AND LEGENDS

Here are four traditional Navajo stories we thought you might enjoy. It is a Navajo custom to tell stories in the winter, because then there is more time and not as much work to do.

The Ye'iitsoh

Judge Sloan's grandfather told him if he was naughty, the Ye'iitsoh (which means the "big monster") would fetch him, carry him off to the mountains, and eat him. Allen was afraid to get into trouble after he heard this story. The story comes from a Navajo legend about the Ye'iitsoh, who took two boys high up onto a mountain in a gunnysack slung over his back.

One day, two boys were told not to wander too far away from home, but they didn't obey and the Ye'iitsoh came and grabbed them. The giant, who was known to eat little kids, put the boys into a sack to take home and eat. Ye'iitsoh started to carry them up the mountain. As he walked along, the boys tore a hole in the sack. Every time the giant rested, the boys would collect rocks to make the sack heavy like them.

On the last stop, before they reached the top of the mountain, the boys got out and

sewed up the hole with the rocks inside. When the Ye'iitsoh reached the top of the mountain and opened the bag, he saw the boys had escaped. The Ye'iitsoh must have looked funny when he realized he had been tricked! The boys felt very lucky to have escaped from the monster, and they didn't wander far from home again.

The Coyote's New Eyes

This story is a favorite with the Sloan children. It talks about a trickster coyote. He does some things he shouldn't, and this teaches us what we shouldn't do.

One day Coyote saw some birds playing. They were throwing their eyes into a tree saying, "Eyes come back to me." When they said that, their eyes came back. Coyote watched them for a moment. Then Coyote got up and said, "Hey, I can do that, it's easy."

The birds just kept saying, "No, it's not for you! You are not like us, you will lose your eyes."

Coyote said, "Only one time, please?" The birds kept saying no, but finally they gave in. The first time Coyote took out his eyes and threw them into the tree, they came back. Coyote asked the birds, "Can I try it again? One more time, please!"

The birds said, "Go ahead, but this is the last time." Coyote threw his eyes into the tree. When he said, "Eyes, come back to me," they didn't come back to him. Coyote kept saying, "Where are my eyes?"

The birds replied, "We'll give you some

new eyes." So the birds all collected some gum pitch from a tree and rolled it into balls like eyeballs and placed them in Coyote's eye sockets.

Coyote continued to beg and beg saying, "Please give me back my real eyes!" Even though he begged and begged, the birds never gave Coyote back his real eyes. When you see a coyote today, this is why his eyes are black. If you look closely at the coyote, you will see tears of sap, from the tar of the tree, running down his face.

The moral of this story is that people should keep their noses out of other people's business.

How Mother Deer Tricked Coyote

One day, Coyote was walking through the bushes and into the trees, minding his own business. On his way through the woods, he saw a couple of baby fawns, but their mother did not see Coyote. Coyote saw all the beautiful spots on the backs of the baby fawns and came closer and closer to get a better look. When the mother deer saw Coyote she got very frightened, but she

did not run away because of her babies. She just watched and waited until Coyote said to her, "You have nice babies!" Still, the deer said nothing. Then Coyote asked, "Where did your babies get those spots?"

The mother replied, "Go home and build a huge fire. Then put your babies close to the fire. The hot sparks that go up will fall down on your babies and make beautiful spots on their coats." So Coyote did just that. He built a big fire and put his babies close to it. But the babies did not get beautiful spots, just burned, singed, and shriveled-up coats. Their mouths looked funny, too. They looked like they were smiling.

Coyote looked at them and said, "You may not have beautiful spots, but you do have beautiful smiles."

From this story we learned that you don't have to do everything someone tells you to do, and you should always look for the good things that happen.

How Fox Stole Fire

A long time ago, before you or anyone here was born, there was a village. Every winter the villagers were very cold, for they were very poor and didn't have any buffalo hides. No one had fire, because fire was high up on the tallest mountain guarded by two giant vultures.

One day Fox got together with all the animals of the forest. "We should get fire! The villagers don't have fur like we do, and they will surely freeze!" said Fox. So the animals decided to work together and steal the fire to help the villagers.

The next day Fox climbed the mountain and grabbed the fire. Then he ran down the hill dodging the vultures all the way. When he got to the bottom, he threw the

fire to Rabbit, and Rabbit threw it to Blue Jay. Then Blue Jay threw it to Squirrel who was sitting in a tree. The fire was too hot for Squirrel's little hands, so he dropped it and the tree swallowed it.

After the vultures left, Fox grabbed some pieces of the tree's bark and rubbed them together very fast and very hard. Sparks flew from the bark and a fire lit.

This is why rubbing two sticks together very fast and very hard can start a fire.

FOOD AND FUN

Dishes made from corn are an important part of the Navajo culture. If you were to come to the Navajo Tribal Fair, you would find many booths serving foods made from corn. We asked Ms. Irene Scott to help us make Navajo food. She is a first grade teacher's assistant at our school and speaks only Navajo. Ms. Marie Enfield, our bilingual teacher, translated what went on, because some students speak only English, and some speak both English and Navajo.

Ms. Scott didn't forget her apron, and you shouldn't either.

Blue Corn Mush

We had a lesson on how to make blue corn mush, a yummy recipe that serves eight people. Boy, we hope we can make it in the future, because we were expert taste-testers this time. Ms. Scott and her son, Ed, showed us how to make this recipe.

You will need:
1 cup juniper ash

1 cup cold water
3 cups boiling water
4 cups blue cornmeal
hot plate
gallon-sized kettle
wire strainer
measuring cup
wire whisk

First, Ed went to the woods and came back with a short branch from a juniper tree. He built a small fire outdoors, set the branch on fire, and held it over a clean flat rock, so he could collect the ashes as they fell off the branch. Then, Ms. Scott put the cornmeal into a pan and set it in a 250° oven for 15 minutes to take all the water out of the corn.

How to make blue corn mush:
1. Heat 3 cups of water in a pot until it boils.
2. Mix ½ cup juniper ash with 1 cup cold water.
3. Scrape the ashes through a metal strainer while you add them to the boiling water. This takes out the lumps. Stir.
4. Add 4 cups of blue cornmeal and stir some more.
5. Boil for 20 minutes, stirring constantly.
6. Take the pan off the stove and then stir some more.

It wasn't long before our classroom was filled with kitchen smells. Ms. Scott stirred the boiling water very gently as she slowly poured the blue cornmeal in. She used a whisk to keep the mush from getting lumpy.

We wrote about what was happening while the mush cooked slowly for about 20 minutes. Ms. Scott kept stirring the mush so it wouldn't burn, and this made it thicken the same on the top and bottom. After the mush was cooked, Ms. Scott took the kettle off the hot plate and let it sit, so the mush could thicken for another five minutes.

At last, the hot mush was served in cups. It vanished as soon as it had cooled enough to eat!

Ms. Scott told us that if you don't use juniper ashes, the mush will turn green instead of blue.

Blue corn mush is excellent with fry bread. If you would like to make fry bread yourself, look for the recipe in the Sioux chapter. Their recipe is a lot like the Navajo recipe, but you might want to follow Ms. Scott's secret for great fry bread. Use Blue Bird flour because it's finer and makes a lighter bread. Try it, you'll love it! You'll be glad you did!

Stick Game

We learned some traditional Navajo games. They are fun to play. You and your friends might like to give this one a try. The stick game is played by the Navajo any time of year. It used to be played by people who herded sheep, but other people play it now, also.

To make the game pieces, you need three pieces of wood cut about three to four inches long. One long side of each piece is rounded like a pipe, and the other is flat. The flat side is blackened. Long ago, people used to blacken the piece with char-

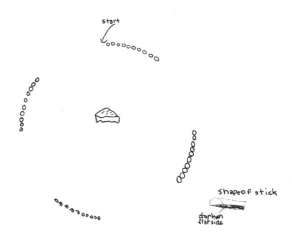

coal, but we usually use a crayon or marker. These pieces of wood are called sticks.

You will also need 40 small stones. To get the game ready, put the stones in a circle and divide the circle into four groups of ten. You can see how we do this by looking at the drawing on this page. Between the four groups of stones should be four large openings. Put a large, flat stone in the middle of the circle.

Now you're ready to play. One at a time, the players drop all three sticks on the flat stone. The way the sticks land tells how many spaces the player moves. A space is

All white or light
☐ ☐ ☐ = 10 points
All black or dark
■ ■ ■ = 5 points
Two black
■ ☐ ■ = 3 points
One black
☐ ☐ ■ = 1 point

Order of blocks doesn't change count. Any two black = 3 points.

the little distance between the stones. The player moves clockwise. This is how to keep score.

If players land on the large spaces between the groups of stones, they go back to the beginning of that group of stones. The first player to go all around the board and get back to where he or she started wins the game.

OUR VISION FOR A BETTER TOMORROW

We, the authors of this chapter, live on the Navajo Reservation in Window Rock, Arizona, and attend fourth and fifth grade at Window Rock Elementary School. Here are some ideas we want to share with you about what it's like to be Navajo.

"It feels good to be Native American, because you get to talk other languages and wear neat Navajo clothing. We also have neat jewelry and shoes. I am proud to be Navajo today and forever."

"I want people to know that we don't wear our Indian clothes all the time anymore. We don't hunt for our food anymore. We live in houses and shop at the store just like you do."

"Some Navajo kids speak English and some speak English and Navajo."

"I want you to know that my favorite foods are pizza and Chinese food. Sometimes I like to eat junk food, but not all the time. Some of my favorite hobbies are collecting things like pencils, erasers, and stamps. My favorite sports are basketball, soccer, and sometimes football."

"It feels good to be Native American. I'm glad that when I go somewhere and people ask who I am, I can say proudly that I am Navajo."

"There are many thoughts that can be said in the Navajo language that cannot be said in English."

"Some of us have learned a lot about our Navajo traditions from our families, and some of us are just learning about our traditions in school."

"Most Navajo do not live in the traditional hogan anymore. Instead, they live in modern houses with big rooms, running water, and electricity, just like you."

"I am a Navajo and I can speak Navajo, too."

We hope you have enjoyed reading our chapter and that you have learned from the story of Judge Sloan. We learned from writing this chapter that all young people need to set goals for themselves and carry them out.

There were a lot of things we wanted you to know about us while we were writing this book, and we hope that you have learned more about our Navajo heritage. We could tell you only some things. We couldn't tell you everything. Remember, you can learn more by studying other books and even taking a trip to visit our reservation.

EXPLORING THE HOPI HERITAGE WITH JOAN TIMECHE

A peaceful people struggling for identity,
Making sure their culture will last.
Building a life in a modern world,
Yet united with their past.

Have you ever been made to feel that you were stupid or not as good as others? Sometimes when people make us feel that way, it is easy to give up and believe them. We met a person who once felt like this, but she fought back in a good way. She decided not to fight with her hands, but by using her brain.

JOAN TIMECHE'S STORY

Joan Timeche began her story by telling us about her high school graduation in May of 1973. She was sitting nervously on the stage waiting for her name to be read and echo through the auditorium. She had worked hard in school and earned the highest grades of all the graduates. Now she had the honor of being the class valedictorian and giving a speech at graduation.

As she sat there, Joan was silently reviewing the speech she had practiced so many times, but something else was stuck in her mind. She remembered the time when

a new girl came to her school in eighth grade. This girl moved to the school in Grand Canyon National Park because her father was the park superintendent. Joan felt that this new student's attitude toward Indians was poor. Although the girl never stated her real opinions, she showed a superior attitude when she was around Indians. That was when Joan decided to do something about it. Being a Hopi Indian, she was determined to prove the new girl wrong!

Joan began to watch what kind of grades the girl got. She noticed she was pretty smart. Joan started to work harder to keep her grades high and became one of the top performers. In fact, she soon had the highest grades in the class. But this was only the beginning. If she wanted to prove the girl wrong, she would have to keep up these good grades for the next four years. She wanted to prove to the girl that Indians aren't dumb!

During her school years, Joan took part in many school activities. In high school, her best friend was a girl named Leslie. She and Leslie liked to do their homework together. They also enjoyed listening to music, taking short hikes in the park and canyon, and just hanging around.

Joan told us that math was her favorite subject and she learned it very easily. Her hardest subject was biology. She thought the biology teacher was mean to the whole class. But she still had to work very hard in every subject to reach her important goal. Even when Joan was getting her good grades and felt very proud of herself, she always remembered an important tradition in Hopi culture. In her culture it is not right to brag or boast about what you have done. So Joan did not tell people about her success of being made valedictorian. In her mind, she felt she proved the girl wrong: Indians are not dumb! Joan also remembers that it was upsetting to her brothers and sisters because others would expect them to do as well as she had.

While she was in school, Ms. Timeche not only earned outstanding grades, but also learned a very valuable lesson that changed her life forever. She learned that she was proud of her heritage and respected her culture. She learned to set goals for herself, knowing that goals worth having require hard work. She realized that she had to make decisions about how she would handle racial teasing.

Because Joan Timeche did so well in high school, the U.S. government paid for her to go to college. When she first started college she studied business at Arizona State University in Tempe, Arizona. Some of the classes there had over 500 people in them! Ms. Timeche remembers feeling very lonesome and homesick because she was so far away from home and had such big classes. She decided to change schools. She went to a smaller school called Northern Arizona University in Flagstaff, Arizona, only 90 miles from her home. She graduated with a bachelor's degree in sociology.

After graduating from college, it was not hard for Ms. Timeche to find work. Her first job was as a counselor for Hopi students who went to school off the reservation. She soon realized that it wasn't a good idea for high school kids to be sent away to boarding schools. When Hopi kids were sent away for as long as nine months at a time to schools in Arizona, California, and Nevada, they started losing the Hopi culture, language, and traditions. Hopi parents decided to start working to get a high school right on the reservation. Ms. Timeche moved into jobs where she helped raise money to build this high school.

Joan Timeche's story is important because she has shown us a better way to handle prejudice and has worked hard to help Native Americans have a better future. When Joan Timeche walked into our classroom we thought she was dressed like a lawyer. She was very nice and very patient. We will try to share the things she told us even though we can't say them in exactly the same wonderful way she did.

Joan Timeche grew up in a very small village on the edge of the Grand Canyon in northwestern Arizona, about three hours from the Hopi reservation. The village was so small that there was only one store, a post office, and a small residential area. Most of the families that lived in the village were white. Indians lived in houses in a separate neighborhood. The houses were considered nice for that time. They had kitchens with running water. Most of them had no bathrooms, so the families used a common bathroom and shower house that they had to walk to.

Perhaps some of you have never been to the Grand Canyon, so we want to tell you a little about it. The Grand Canyon is a spectacular gorge, almost 280 miles long,

that was carved by the Colorado River. The canyon is almost a mile deep in some places. It became a national park in 1919. Visitors come from all over the world to see the Grand Canyon. Joan and her family enjoyed living close by. When she was young, she would watch the beautiful sunsets over the canyon. She remembers seeing the sun going down and the sky changing from yellow to pink to orange to red, and then darkness. Joan's father, Gilbert Timeche, was a painter and her mother, Mary, who is deceased, was a housekeeper at a hotel near the Grand Canyon.

The Timeche family practiced many customs of their culture. They ate traditional Hopi dishes like mutton and hominy stew, call Noq kwi vi. Mr. and Mrs. Timeche taught their two oldest children to speak Hopi before they started school. But when the children entered school, they had a difficult time learning how to speak English. Mr. and Mrs. Timeche then decided to teach the rest of their children how to speak English instead of Hopi, so school wouldn't be so hard for them.

Joan's weekends with her family were different from most of her friends' weekends. Every weekend her parents loaded all the kids in the station wagon and drove three hours to the reservation to visit her grandparents. Joan didn't like this very much. She would rather have stayed at home in the Grand Canyon Village playing with her friends and going to birthday parties. But she didn't get to do that.

At that time on the Hopi reservation, during the 1960s, the houses had thick stone

walls, dirt floors, no running water, and no electricity. Even though Joan didn't like the hard work there, her grandparents appreciated the help. One of Joan's chores on the reservation was to get water at the artesian well. She and one of her brothers or sisters would pull a little red wagon with two big tin milk cans up to the well. They would put the bucket, attached to the rope, down in the well. When both cans were full, they would pull the little red wagon back to her grandparents' house. The Hopi on the reservation tried to conserve their water. They had to be very careful not to use too much when they washed dishes and did other chores.

The reservation houses were heated by burning wood or coal. Finding and chopping wood was a tough job and belonged to the men and boys, but the whole family helped gather it. So there was often hard work to be done on Joan's weekends to make sure her grandparents had enough water, wood, and coal to last the week.

After weekend chores were done the girls played with bone dolls in the soft sand. The girls learned how to use their imaginations by playing with these simple toys for hours. The bones for these dolls came from a stew that the family made. There were many sizes of bones and each one stood for a member of the family or a piece of furniture. The biggest bones would be the mother and father and the smaller bones would be the children. If there was a tiny bone, it could be the baby. Sometimes Joan and her sisters took old tin cans and pretended they were cars for the bone dolls and drove them on the sand. They also made match boxes into beds. Other little bones, cans, and boxes were used as furniture. They piled up rocks to make the walls for the bone dolls' houses. Ms. Timeche told us that playing bone dolls was fun and a lot like playing with Barbies.

Ms. Timeche is a role model for many people because of how hard she worked at getting her education and all the time she has given to helping the Hopi. She spent eight years as Director of Education helping children to see that no matter what kind of job you want to do, school is important for everyone. Ms. Timeche has won two awards, so we are not the only ones who think she is a great person. She was chosen Hopi of the Year in 1993 for teaching others about the Hopi's needs and cultural beliefs. She also won the Petra Foundation award in 1989 for fighting for human rights.

Ms. Timeche is a member of the board of directors of the Hopi Indian Credit Association. This made her interested in business. Today she works at Northern Arizona University in Flagstaff, where she is the Pro-

Joan Timeche

gram Director of the Center for American Indian Economic Development. She helps Native Americans who want to start businesses on Arizona's Indian reservations. She encourages them and teaches them how to raise money for their businesses. She also helps them understand how to run a business, and how to obey tribal and state laws. She does this because she wants her people to be able to do things for themselves and succeed as Native Americans, and be able to earn a good living, too.

Joan Timeche's Personal Statement

As I look back on all my experiences and challenges, I realize that I am fortunate to have been able to accomplish what I have in my life. I've learned that I can make a difference in the quality of life I lead.

If you have a strong sense of who you are as a person, your values and beliefs, you will be better able to deal with life's challenges. So the next time you're faced with a negative remark or a circumstance that hurts you, instead of allowing it to pull you down, be strong inside and figure out how to make the best of it. Remember that no matter what you have to face, you are responsible for yourself. After all, you have to live with yourself and your actions.

It is important to be proud of who you are. Learn as much as you can about your heritage. We all come from rich cultural backgrounds, no matter the color of our skin. If your first language is not English, learn your language and help preserve it for future generations. The one major regret I have is that I do not speak the Hopi language fluently. When I think about the people I admire, I usually find that they know a lot about their heritage and are fluent in both their native tongue and English. I believe this gives them a tremendous advantage in dealing with life.

If I could leave you with only one message, it would be to believe in yourself. Only you have power over yourself. Set goals for yourself, figure out a way to achieve them, and work at them. Some goals take longer than others, but I know that you can do just about anything you set your mind to.

THE FAMILY

We were very lucky to have met and learned so much from Ms. Timeche. She shared something that is even more important than being valedictorian or having an important job—she introduced us to Briana Tewawina, her six-year-old daughter. Briana is a very pretty little girl with long, shiny hair. She has a very pretty Hopi name, Yoyokmana, which means Rain Girl. She was born in Tuba City, Arizona. Now she lives with her mom and her grandpa in Flagstaff, Arizona, and they also keep the family home in Old Oraibi, located on the Hopi reservation. Old Oraibi is the oldest continuously inhabited village in all of North America. It is believed to be over 800 years old!

At first Briana was shy but then she told us about some of her favorite things. Her favorite color is purple and her favorite food is cheese pizza. We asked her what her

Briana Timeche

favorite Hopi food is and she told us Noq kwi vi, which is hominy stew. Instead of playing with bone dolls like her mother, Briana likes to play with Barbie dolls.

Briana is in first grade at DeMiguel Elementary School in Flagstaff. She told us that sometimes she doesn't like school very much because the other kids tease her. Briana told us that she has a friend and at recess time they like to play Barbies on the playground and they also like to chase the boys. Her favorite Hopi dance to watch is the butterfly dance.

We enjoyed meeting Briana. We hope that she will like school better as she gets older and will learn some of the same lessons her mom did: to never give up, to set goals, and not to believe in racial teasing.

We have already told you about Joan, so now we're going to tell you a little bit about her brothers and sisters, Teresa, Gregory, Cindy, Mike, and Daran. Even though they live far apart in Arizona, Utah, and Alaska, they all try to spend time with each other. They go back as often as they can to the family house on the Hopi reservation where they used to visit their grandparents. All of Joan's brothers and sisters live and work off the reservation, but still take time to help with family responsibilities like planting corn, beans, and watermelons. They take care of the family's orchards that grow apricots, apples, pears, and peaches. Everyone helps pick the fruits and vegetables during harvest time.

Teresa is Joan's older sister and she lives in Tuba City, Arizona. She has an interesting job teaching parenting classes at Parents Anonymous, a company that helps Hopi and Navajo parents and their children. Teresa has two children, Jeanette, who is 23, and Jon, who is 21. Her children are half Hopi and Teresa works very hard at teaching them about their Hopi heritage. She also has two grandchildren.

Greg, Joan's oldest brother, lives in Alaska with his wife, Terry, and their children, Daniel and Jessica. Greg works at Denali National Park near Mt. McKinley. Many people want to visit Mt. McKinley, but Greg gets to work there! He is in charge of keeping the heat going in all of the park buildings. For hobbies, Greg like to fish and hunt. Since he lives so far away from the family and the reservation, it is hard for him to attend Hopi celebrations with his kids. But

he still tries to do his best at sharing what he knows about Hopi traditions. Greg and his family can only go back home to Arizona every three years because it costs so much money to get there. When he does go home he spends his time helping to prepare the family fields for planting and working on the family home.

Cindy is Joan's younger sister. She lives and works in Tempe, Arizona, which is near Phoenix. Her daughter, Devonna, is 17 years old and can't wait to go to college! Cindy recently became a guardian for Tara, her 14-year-old cousin. The family often travels to the reservation to participate in religious and cultural activities. Cindy works at the post office. She likes to read and lis-

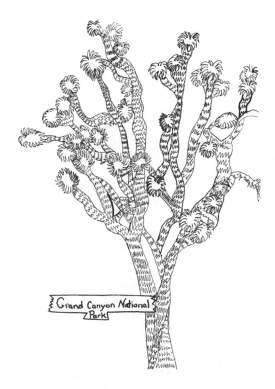

Grand Canyon National Park

ten to good music. She especially likes to go to concerts and hear live music.

Mike is Joan's second brother. He lives near where his family lived when he was young, in Grand Canyon Village. He and his wife Terry, who is also a Hopi, have a growing family: Merreyna is seven, Megan is four, Marissa is two, and Morgan is the new baby. Mike has a great job at the Grand Canyon National Park. He helps with the mule trains that carry supplies down to the bottom of the canyon, so the workers can fix the trails.

Mike also takes a lot of responsibility for the family home on the reservation. He spends most of his free time there planting and tending his family's fields and his wife's family's fields. He and his family take part in many Hopi religious and cultural activities. Mike also has an interesting hobby. He carves Kachina dolls and sells them to make extra money for his family.

Daran is Joan's youngest brother. He lives in Orem, Utah, with his wife Priscilla and their four children. Aneisha, the baby, is only one. Joshua is three, and the two girls,Cherrell and Griselda, are five. Daran works in the meat department at Albertson's grocery store. He also is very good at carving and carves Kachina dolls to sell. Daran tries to teach his children about the Hopi heritage and Priscilla shares what she knows about her heritage, which is Navajo.

THE HOPI NATION

The Hopi Indians have lived in northeastern Arizona for more than two thousand years.

HOPI NATION

Their houses are made from stone, not adobe. Their villages are located on top of mesas called First Mesa, Second Mesa, and Third Mesa. A mesa is a flat-topped mountain or hill. Here you will find Old Oraibi, where the Timeche family has its home.

The Hopi have great respect for nature. They work hard to take care of nature and keep things in balance. They have learned to use water wisely to be able to farm in a hot, dry climate. Even long ago, the Hopi men were farmers. They worked the fields, planting and tending the crops. The corn that was planted in April was ready to harvest in July. Other crops would be planted in May, such as beans, squash, and more corn. Cotton was also grown. The men raised the cotton and then used it to make cloth for clothing and blankets. Hopi men hunted for rabbits and other small animals around their villages. They traveled into the nearby mountains to hunt antelope and deer.

Hopi women did a lot of work. They took care of the children and prepared the family's food. They had to prepare the corn for cooking by shelling it. Some of the corn was ground into a fine meal. The women also made pottery for cooking and carrying water.

Families are very important to the Hopi people. A man becomes part of his wife's family when he marries, and children belong to the mother's clan. The members of each clan follow certain rules and help each other in times of trouble.

The Hopi have a strong belief in spirits. Religious practices link the people to spirits and ancestors through prayers, offerings, and special ceremonies. Many ceremonies are held in a kiva. Even the Kachinas offer their dances to the spirits in the kiva. The Hopi teach that Kachinas are living spirits and messengers between the Hopi gods and the Hopi people. The Kachinas come between the months of December and July in ceremonies that help bring enough rain to grow good crops.

When Hopi children are ten or a little older, they are initiated into the first religious society at a special ceremony during the Bean Dance. Other ceremonies are held throughout the year for weddings, births, and funerals.

The Hopi have a custom of taking good care of guests and treating them well. When the Hopi first discovered the Spanish camping near their homeland, they made them feel welcome. The friendship only went bad when the Spanish kept asking for more and more crops and other stuff.

Hopi means "good, cooperation, peaceful and respectful." The Hopi people work together for harmony in the world and with other people. They believe they share the earth with all living things and the spiritual world. They try to blend the old and new together while keeping a strong tie with their family or clan. Many Hopi live off of the reservation and have to work very hard to carry on Hopi traditions.

HISTORY TIMELINE

1540 The Hopi discovered a group of Spaniards below their mesa cliffs.

around 1600 Many Hopi were killed after more Spaniards invaded their territory.

1629-41 Catholic Franciscan missionaries camped on Hopi land and learned to speak the Hopi language. They tried to make the Hopi become Catholic. The Hopi traded with the Spanish for metal tools, new crops, and livestock.

1680 The Hopi drove the missionaries away and went back to their own beliefs. They moved their villages to three mesas to keep away from other people.

1700s The Hopi successfully fought off attacks by Spanish invaders.

1821 The Republic of Mexico claimed Hopi territory.

1824 The U.S. Bureau of Indian Affairs was established to oversee laws and programs for Native Americans.

1848 The Hopi territory became part of the United States after the Mexican-American War.

1850 The Bureau of Indian Affairs set up regional headquarters in Santa Fe, New Mexico. The Hopi started working with this office to stop the Navajo and Ute raids against them.

1851-52 The U.S. government built Fort Defiance in western New Mexico. Soldiers from the fort were sent to help the Hopi defend themselves against the Navajo and Ute.

1853-54 A smallpox epidemic broke out and killed hundreds of Hopi. (This disease was brought by Europeans when they came to America.) During the same year, there was not enough rain and all the crops died. Many Hopi starved to death. For example, the population of Oraibi went from 800 people to about 200 people.

1864-68 The terrible Navajo raids continued. The U.S. ordered Kit Carson to round up all the Navajo and take them as prisoners near Fort Sumner in southeast New Mexico. Many Hopi and about a hundred Ute scouts helped.

1882 President Chester A. Arthur signed an order that made a reservation where Hopi and other Indians could live. The reservation did not include all of the Hopi lands.

Early 1900s Oil was found on the Hopi reservation.

1934 The Indian Reorganization Act was passed. The Hopi voted to accept this act in 1935. They drafted a constitution that formed a tribal council and court. From then on, the Hopi had their own democratic government.

1950s The government built many roads, dams, and wells on the Hopi reservation.

1961 The Hopi Tribal Council decided to let outside companies dig for oil, gas, and minerals on the reservation.

1974 The U.S. Congress split the Hopi reservation land between the Hopi and Navajo people through the Navajo-Hopi Settlement Act.

Today Many Hopi raise livestock, farm, or work at other jobs. Some live in modern Hopi villages and some live off the reservation. Hopi art is popular and some Hopi artists design silver jewelry, carve Kachina dolls, and make other things to sell.

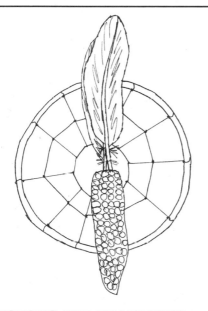

CUSTOMS AND TRADITIONS

The Hopi people are a mix of old and new. They have kept old traditions throughout generations and have learned new ways. These are some of the traditions that the Timeche family carries on today.

Kachina Dance
We were lucky that the Timeche family invited us to a very special ceremony, a Long-hair Kachina Dance. We went to Old Oraibi to see the ceremony. The houses there have thick stone walls which make them cool in the summer and keep them warm in the winter.

We met the people from the village at the village square to see the male Kachinas and the female Katsinmanas dance. The Kachinas danced, sang, and made wonderful music. They followed a leader who told them where to move next. The leader sprinkled cornmeal on each Kachina. This symbolized feeding them. We saw many Kachinas and a few Katsinmanas. To be respectful, picture-taking is not allowed.

Clans
As a Hopi, Joan Timeche is a member of a clan. A clan is a group of families who take care of a specific responsibility of Hopi life. Joan belongs to the Ma'asaw Clan. The Ma'asaw Clan's responsibility is to be the guardian of this world. This clan is sometimes called the Fire Clan because it is seen as the keeper of the fire. Another clan, the Badger Clan, is responsible for taking care of the sacred spruce. These are the names of some other Hopi clans: Bear, Snake, Water, Fire, Sun, Eagle, Wild Mustard, Deer, and Flute.

Birth

The time after a Hopi baby is born is a happy and busy time. It is when babies become members of their mother's clan. The twentieth day after the baby's birth is the day of the naming ceremony. About one hour before the sun comes up on that day, the baby's aunts from the father's side of the family come to the house. Then the grandmother and aunts wash the mother's and baby's hair in two ways. One way is to clean it, and the other is part of a ceremony. When the baby is washed and dressed by the baby's grandmother from the father's side of the family, each of the aunts gives the baby a Hopi name and a shawl or blanket. They also give the baby's mother a shawl or blanket. One of Joan's Hopi names is Paamansi. This stands for the water lily, a thing of beauty.

At sunrise, the same grandmother takes the baby and his mother outside to meet and welcome the sun, and to say prayers for a healthy and successful life. When they return from the sunrise, the baby is given his first solid food, like piki, which is a very thin bread. By this time the baby is ready for some milk and a nap. Then the baby's mother, grandmother, and aunts eat, too.

When the guests leave, the baby's mother gives them cornmeal, piki, and pastries to thank them for naming her child, bringing gifts, and being willing to help raise the baby. Then the mother's family invites the entire village to eat at their home. That way, the people of the village can see the baby and the new blankets, and learn the baby's new names. There is another meal at noon that the village is also invited to. They eat traditional Hopi food like sheep's intestines and blood cake.

Weddings

The Hopi have many wedding customs. Many Hopi families attend weddings on the reservation. Joan explained to us what happens at a Hopi wedding. Both the bride and groom have to be Hopi, and they must come from different clans. A Hopi wedding has three parts.

The first part is the engagement ceremony where the woman claims the man she wants to marry by having her aunt take her to his village, where she gives him sweet cornmeal dough and some food.

The second part of the wedding is the actual wedding ceremony. A long time ago, the bride and her aunt would stay with the groom's family until the two wedding robes were woven. This could take as little as two weeks, or even up to one month or more. The bride was expected to cook and grind blue corn for all her in-laws, because they helped her to prepare the wedding clothes. On the wedding day, the groom's family dresses the bride, and the bride's family brings them a gift of blue cornmeal. The bride's wedding outfit is a black wool manta (Hopi dress), one of her new wedding robes, a belt, and buckskin moccasins. The bride makes piki bread and serves it with hominy stew at the wedding feast.

The last part of the wedding is when the bride's family pays back the groom's family for making the wedding robes. Her family gives his family more blue cornmeal and specially woven plaques. The time it takes to make the plaques depends on how good the weaver is. It takes an expert weaver just a few days, while it can take a beginning weaver several months or even a year to weave the plaque. Altogether, you can see that the whole wedding ceremony can last for several years!

STORIES AND LEGENDS

Stories have always been a fun part of different heritages. It is the same for the Hopi. Even though stories are important to the Hopi people, they aren't told in the summer because there is too much work in the fields. Stories are told when there is snow on the mountains. We were happy to have Briana's grandfather share a Hopi story with us. We think Mr. Timeche is a great storyteller. We think you will enjoy how we have retold his story.

The Lizard and the Sparrow Hawk

There was once a lizard and a sparrow hawk who lived in the hot dry desert on the Third Mesa of the Hopi. Food was really hard to find for the hawk, who had to search with his sharp eyes. The lizard couldn't see very clearly and was not too smart. But he loved to tease and annoy the sparrow hawk. The lizard lived in his own little crack in the rock. He would get bored with nothing to do, so he would go outside and dance and sing.

One day the lizard was feeling really brave, so he decided he would tease the sparrow hawk. While he was dancing he sang, "You would catch me if you thought you could, 'cause I am juicy and very good."

Just as the sparrow hawk was about to swoop down and catch him, the lizard would rush back and slip into his little crack in the rock. Sometimes the hawk would almost catch the lizard's skinny little tail that squeezed out of the crack. The lizard teased him over and over again, until the sparrow hawk got fed up with the lizard and came up with a plan. He went out on the mesa and found a white rock that looked like a bird. He put it on the ledge where he usually stood. The lizard came out to do his dance as usual. Of course, he thought the white rock was the sparrow hawk, but by this time the sparrow hawk was flying swiftly overhead. The sparrow hawk swooped down on the lizard and grabbed him up with his talons. The sparrow hawk took the lizard up to his nest, high on the mesa ledge. He was upset to discover that this lizard was the skinniest thing he had ever seen. But he made an afternoon snack out of the lizard anyway.

Of course, the moral of this story is to never show off because there is always someone who is quicker and hungrier than you are.

Winter Rabbit Hunts

This story is one of Joan Timeche's favorites. She hoped we would retell it for you, and even gave us a book to help us do that.

I woke up to a nice winter snow. I jumped out of bed and got dressed as fast as I could. I looked out the window and the plaza was covered with fresh white snow.

My parents were already up and my brother still lay cozy in his bed fast asleep. I was so excited because I had wonderful plans: I was going rabbit hunting with my father and other men and boys from the village. When I went into the kitchen my parents were eating their breakfast and talking about the hunt. My boots and my dad's boots were sitting next to the fire to get warm. They were made of lamb skin. Near the door was a bag with dried peaches, ground piki, and the other things we would need while we were away on the hunt.

After my dad finished eating, we went down the mesa trail out to the fields where there were lots of cottontails and jack rabbits to hunt. We met some men and boys waiting by a nice warm fire. My father showed me how to do a prayer using bits of grasses over the fire. The prayer was to insure a good winter hunt with plentiful amounts of rabbit and other game for the food supply.

FOOD AND FUN

Every culture has its own special foods. The Hopi people have grown corn and used it as one of their main foods for hundreds of years. We learned two Hopi corn recipes that were fun and easy to make.

Blue Marbles

Blue marbles are one of Briana's favorite foods. They are usually eaten for breakfast. This recipe makes enough to serve one person. Just wait until you taste them!

You will need:
½ cup blue cornmeal
2 heaping teaspoons chamisa ashes or
   baking powder
8 tablespoons boiling water
1 tablespoon sugar (if you want)

How to make blue marbles:
1. Mix 2 tablespoons boiling water with chamisa ash (or baking powder). Put aside.
2. Add the sugar to the blue cornmeal.
3. Stir 5 tablespoons of water into the sugar/cornmeal mixture, so it is like a cookie dough.

4. Pour about 2 tablespoons or more of the ash-water through a strainer into the cornmeal. The ashes will turn it light blue. Be careful not to add too much!

5. Make little balls out of the cornmeal, ashes, and boiling water (about the size of marbles).

6. Drop the balls into about 2 cups boiling water. Cook for 10 minutes.

7. Serve the marbles in the cooking water. You also might want to add dried onions, fresh or dried chilies, beef strips, or fried salt pork. You could also eat them with mutton and hominy stew.

Dried Corn

The Hopi use dried corn to make many different things, like the hominy recipe that comes after this one.

You will need:
several ears of corn
water
large enamel or glass pan

How to dry corn:
1. Take the husks off the ears of corn.
2. Let the corn sit out and air-dry for about two weeks, or until the kernels are hard and totally dry.
3. Put the corn away until it is going to be used.

Hominy

How to make hominy:
1. Take the dried corn kernels off of the cob. The Hopi do this by hitting a corn cob against the dried ear of corn, but this takes a lot of practice. It is okay to rub the kernels off the cob with your hands.

2. Separate the good kernels of corn from the bad ones. Hopi women do this by using sifter baskets, but you can use your hands.

3. Boil the dried corn in an enamel pot for at least two hours, or until the corn starts to get soft. Add chamisa ash or baking soda to help take off the hull (kernel skin). Keep boiling until the kernels get firm and the hulls have come off.

4. Take the hominy (corn) out of the pan to wash it. Rinse it several times to get rid of the chamisa ash or baking soda water, and rub the kernels gently to make sure all the hulls have come off.

5. When the hominy is washed, you are now ready to make Hominy Stew. Look at the next recipe.

Hominy Stew

This food is often served to guests. We were honored to be invited to the Timeche home to eat hominy stew with them. This recipe will feed about ten hungry kids.

You will need:
2 pounds mutton or beef backbones, cut
  into 1-inch pieces
water
10 cups hominy (fresh, dried, or frozen)
1 tablespoon salt

How to make hominy stew:
1. Put the meat in a pot, cover with water, and stir in the salt.
2. Put a lid on the pot and cook over high heat for about two hours or until

the meat gets tender.

3. Add the hominy that has already been cooked.

4. Cook the meat and hominy in a covered pot all night, until the hominy and meat become soft. Now it is ready to serve.

Bone Dolls

Years ago, in all heritages, children's toys were very simple because people could not get to stores very often, and the stores didn't sell many toys. Today, Briana plays with Barbie dolls like most other Hopi girls. It might be fun some summer day to play like the Hopi children did years ago.

The Hopi girls used to play with bone dolls. We have learned that sometimes boys used to play with bone dolls, but they would never admit it. This is how you can make some bone dolls. When you cook

meat for stew, the meat falls off the bones. You then take these bones, wash them, and use them to play a game of bone dolls.

There is no special way to play bone dolls. Hopi kids like Joan Timeche often played with the dolls and had them do things just like their real family. This game actually teaches the kids the responsibilities of adult life. It shows the kids what it will be like when they are grown up and have children of their own.

Hopi boys played some different games from the girls. They sometimes pretended to be Kachinas and danced. They also played games with a dart or a shuttlecock, which is like the birdie batted back and forth in badminton.

The game of shuttlecock is very old. Visitors to the pueblos saw people playing shuttlecock in the late 1800s. In those

days, they played with a hoop made by wrapping cornhusks around native spun white wool cord. They made the darts with corncobs and feathers.

Shuttlecock

Dr. Willard Gilbert, a Hopi who works at Northern Arizona University, told us how to make shuttlecocks so we could use them to play a game called Hula Throw. Dr. Gilbert said he used to play this game when he was on the reservation. Here are the directions for making a shuttlecock so you can play too.

You will need:
1 leaf from a cornhusk
1 teaspoon of sand or dirt
1 small piece of plastic wrap
2 or 3 feathers

How to make a shuttlecock:
1. Cut two pieces off the cornhusk leaf that are about 6 inches long and 1 inch wide. Cut one piece off the corn husk leaf that is about ¼ inch wide and 7 inches long.
2. Take the two bigger pieces of cornhusk and make a cross with these.
3. Next, take a teaspoon of sand or soil, wrap it in a small square of plastic wrap, and wad it up into a ball. We used sand in ours.
4. Place the sand ball in the center of the cornhusk cross.

Turns out to Look Like this

5. Fold up the "arms" of the cornhusk cross, so they meet above the sandball. (See illustration.)

6. Take the thin piece of cornhusk and tie it near the center to hold the other pieces together.

7. Take two or three feathers and place them near the center.

Now you are ready to get an old hula hoop and play a game with your new shuttlecock. First, form two teams with the same number of people on each. Have the two teams stand in two lines about ten feet apart (see illustration). Second, pick a volunteer to be the judge. The judge will roll the hoop down the center of the two teams.

Third, decide which team will go first and how many turns you want to have in a game. We recommend ten turns per game. Fourth, the judge rolls the hoop down the center and the whole team tries to throw their shuttlecocks through the hoop as it rolls in front of them. Team members must not get out of their line. The judge gives the team one point for each shuttlecock that makes it through the hoop. Then the other team does the same thing. The judge should say the score out loud after each turn.

The winner is the team that has the most points.

Remember, there are many books with more recipes, games, and crafts of the Hopi people. We hope you will get some of these books from your library and learn more about the Hopi culture.

OUR VISION FOR A BETTER TOMORROW

We learned a lot of things while working on this chapter that we wanted to share with you. Some of us learned more about our own heritage; others learned about the Hopi heritage for the first time.

We found out that the Hopi people are a mix of old and new. They have kept their old traditions but have learned new things and made our world better. The Hopi are people who never seem to give up and always keep trying. By helping with our book we feel that Hopi people have helped us work to fight racism. We feel hopeful that by writing this chapter we can make a difference.

We all found out together that the most important thing is what is on the inside of a person. This is what counts. If you spend time learning about other cultures and not just assuming things about them, you will learn a lot you didn't know. Everyone is the same, and everyone has feelings. Even if their beliefs or language are different, that doesn't give you the right to be mean to them or make fun of them. Their beliefs are just as important to them as yours are to you.

We hope you have had as much fun as we did exploring the Hopi heritage.

EXPLORING THE YAKAMA HERITAGE WITH FRANCES SMISCON

A young Yakama woman that lives today,
Passing on traditions in an honorable way.
For her God and family are number one,
Frances Smiscon is always busy and having fun.

Frances Smiscon is a real team player in more ways than one. She works on many different teams. You might find her performing with her dance group, acting with her drama troupe, playing on a sports team, or working for the Wapato Indian Club. She is only fourteen years old, but she knows what is important and stands up for what she believes. Frances comes from a family that is always working to make the world a better place. We are proud to share Frances Smiscon's story and the life of her Yakama family with you. Our story about Frances starts with a busy night at the Smiscon house.

FRANCES SMISCON'S STORY

Frances is laughing and talking with her mother in the kitchen. They are busy cooking a spaghetti dinner for the whole family (all eight of them). Frances' dad watches over baby Clifton and her younger brothers and sisters. Five-year-old Jim plays with his Teenage Mutant Ninja Turtles, and his little sister Denise sits glued to Barney on TV. Twelve-year-old Tracey, the next oldest sister, enjoys her Sega Gamegear, while Stephanie sits drawing a picture for her second-grade book-sharing assignment. It isn't long before the whole family holds hands around the dinner table and thanks God for their food and all the blessings in their life.

This is just a normal evening at Frances' house. With homework, chores, school, and sports, Frances and her family are always busy. Like other American families, the Smiscons are proud of their happy family and work hard to keep it that way.

Because she is the oldest child in the family, Frances works extra hard on her school work, so she can go to a university someday and become a top business person. Frances is in eighth grade at Wapato Middle School. Her favorite classes are P.E. and math. Like a lot of kids, Frances loves music, sports, talking on the phone, and going to slumber parties. But spending time with baby Clifton is also very important to her. She enjoys responsibility, too, and often cooks many different foods like fry bread, potatoes, and steak for her family. As you can see, Frances is always busy.

Frances feels very lucky to have a sister just 13 months younger than she is. The

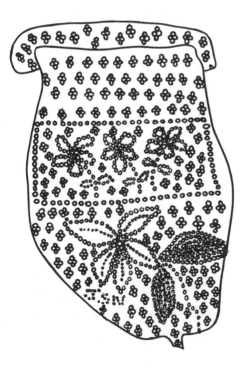

girls are not just sisters, they're best friends, too. They like to go to movies together and play basketball and softball. As you may have guessed, they go to the same school and belong to the same dance group.

School is fun for Frances and Tracey. Wapato Middle School has 800 sixth, seventh, and eighth graders, who come from all different heritages like their teachers. Everyone at the school works very hard at respecting and understanding the differences between each other. To help this along, the school puts on a cultural unity fair every year with foods and displays, and special performances from many cultures. Last year, Mrs. Decoteau, a Yakama teacher at the school, taught Frances and other students to do traditional beadwork. They made small, beaded pouches that look like little purses, and they sold them at Unity Fair.

One important way Frances and Tracey work to help all kinds of people be friends is through the Wapato Indian Club at school. This club has 194 members, and you do not have to be Native American to join. If you want to learn more about Native American culture, and if you are willing to work for brotherhood and goodwill to all people, you can be a club member. It's that easy. All club members believe and practice respect and appreciation for their elders and Mother Earth. Mother Earth means all of nature—animals, birds, water, and plants.

Frances is in charge of all activities for the Wapato Indian Club. She puts together field trips, benefit performances, and other excit-

Frances Smiscon in her traditional dress

ing things like the school's roller skating party that the club sponsored. She also arranged for her dance group to perform at a mall. Both Frances and Tracey have traveled and performed in many different places. Frances is a traditional dancer and Tracey is a Fancy Dancer. When they perform they wear colorful traditional regalia, or outfits, called wing dresses.

When Frances got the news one summer that her dance team had been invited to perform at Disney World, she was thrilled. But the invitation meant she would have to make a very tough decision. She had hoped to take a special summer job working with kids. This dream was too important to give up, and Frances decided not to go on the trip herself. Instead, she helped organize the whole trip because she felt that the group could really teach others about Yakama traditions! To help pay for the trip, the club had fund-raisers. Some of these fund-raisers were benefit dances. The dancers would put a shawl on the floor for people to toss money in. At one of the benefits, the club made $400 doing the shawl dance.

In the summer of 1994, Tracey and forty-nine members of the Indian Club went on a dance tour to Georgia and Florida. Ten adults went on the trip to keep an eye on the kids. Frances' grandmother, Mrs. Marie Shilow, happened to be one of these chaperones. Frances was very happy that her sister Tracey and her grandma would represent their family on the Disney World trip. The group danced first in Atlanta, Georgia. Then they went on to Tampa, Florida, where they danced at a meeting for music teachers from all over the world. Performing was lots of fun, and it was really amazing to dance for all kinds of people.

Before the big dance performance in Epcot Center at Disney World, the whole group took a side trip to the Gulf of Mexico and got to play in the ocean. On a second side trip, the group toured the Kennedy Space Center and went inside a model of the first spaceship that landed on

Frances (front row, second from left) with her drama troupe at the Yakama National Summer Youth Employment Program

the moon. The whole dance tour was lots of fun, and it gave the Wapato Indian Club a chance to meet and learn about people from the southern United States and Mexico. Best of all, it taught the people they performed for a little about the Yakama of Washington state.

Frances loved hearing about the neat trip from Tracey and her grandma. She wasn't sorry about staying home because her summer was special, too. While the club was away, Frances was working in the drama troupe with the Yakama Nation Summer Youth Employment Program. She worked with about a dozen other teenagers. The group performed skits for children about staying away from alcohol, drugs, and smoking, and about not talking to strangers.

Frances had a great time, and she hopes that doing her summer job helped some little kids make some big decisions.

Maybe one reason Frances is such a great team player is that her parents have always encouraged her to take part in all kinds of sports. The Smiscon family believes that sports really teach people how to cooperate and get along. Frances plays volleyball, basketball, and softball, but softball is her favorite. Frances told us a great softball story.

In the spring of 1992, Frances got an unexpected call from

John Cozzens

her cousin. The regular catcher for her cousin's softball team was sick, and her cousin wanted to know if Frances would travel to Oregon with the team and fill in. Frances thought it sounded like a lot of fun to play in a championship tournament and said yes right away. What looked like nothing more than an invitation to help out her cousin and have fun turned out to be a big turning point in life for Frances. Here's what happened.

It was the last inning, and Frances' team was losing 7 to 1. Frances caught a foul ball for the third out, and then her team was up to bat for the last time. It looked impossible. And then her team scored a run…and then another…and another, on and on, until finally her team had tallied up seven runs to win the tournament by one single point! The final score was 8 to 7. Frances will never forget this special game. It taught her that no matter how far behind you are in anything, you always have a chance to come back and win.

Frances Smiscon's Personal Statement

I have learned not to judge others without getting to know them first. I have many friends from different backgrounds. They are African American, Hispanic, Asian, and Caucasian. If someone teases me because I am different from them, I try to ignore them. When my friends get teased, I tell them, "Just play the game and ignore that kind of stuff."

Although I am young, I know I can do a lot of things. I can influence many people by what I say and by what I do. I try to be a good example and show respect for my family, my school, and my heritage. Always remember to try hard and do your best. If you work hard to make your dreams come true, you will be a success in life.

THE FAMILY

All together there are five children in Frances' family. Tracey is a seventh-grader and has been on the honor roll all year because she got good grades. Math is her

Tracey Smiscon does a Fancy Dance

favorite subject. She plays the clarinet in the Wapato Middle School Marching Band. In her free time, she enjoys shooting hoops with Frances and her friends. When Tracey grows up she would like to go to college and be an engineer or a math teacher. We think she will choose one of these jobs because she's so good at math.

Tracey is also very good at sports. She plays basketball, softball, and track. In track, she runs the 200 meter dash. On her softball team, she likes to pitch most of all. Even though Tracey plays a lot of sports, her favorite is basketball. She is a forward on the middle school basketball team, and one time she scored 38 points in one game!

The rest of the Smiscon family enjoys playing sports in their free time. Stephanie, in second grade, plays t-ball. Jim and Denise like to watch the others play and can hardly

Stephanie Smiscon in her traditional dress

wait to play when they get a little older and go to school. Baby Clifton just gets to go to everyone else's games. The older girls are really lucky because Mr. and Mrs. Smiscon coach their teams. Both parents play softball and bowl in a league, too. Mr. Smiscon has a big collection of sports cards.

Even though this family loves sports, they believe that getting an education is most important because they know that kids are the leaders of the future. Frances' parents both work at the Yakama Tribal School. Mr. Smiscon is in charge of the school buses, and Mrs. Smiscon makes sure that employees and bills all get paid. Working at the Yakama Tribal School is more than an ordinary job because this special school works hard to keep kids from dropping out of school.

The Yakama Tribal School has 105 students in the seventh through the twelfth grades. It offers many special classes. Some students choose to take agriculture classes and grow plants in the greenhouse. In other classes, kids can learn about their culture and their native language or take field trips to the mountains to dig for roots. For kids who like to make things, Native American art classes do projects like jewelry and dream catchers, a kind of good luck charm. Some of the seventh and eighth graders from the Yakama Tribal School helped write this chapter.

It is easy for Mr. and Mrs. Smiscon to go to work because they are working for something they believe in. They also know their young children are being well cared for while they work by Mrs. Smiscon's mother, Mrs. Marie Shilow.

Marie Smiscon and her grandchildren, Jim, baby Clifton, and Denise

Mrs. Shilow is a very important person in the Smiscon family. Because Frances told us her grandma is one of her heroes, who has taught her a lot about her culture, we would like you to know her story.

Marie Shilow was born August 13, 1926. There were nine kids in her family. They lived on the Yakama reservation in the state of Washington. Her dad used to chase after the wild horses that lived on the prairies south of the town of Toppenish. This was one of his favorite things to do. When he caught the horses, he would train them to get used to a rope and saddle. Then they would be ready to sell to farmers.

When she was growing up, Marie's family went to Celilo Falls on the Columbia River to catch salmon. They dried and stored the salmon they caught until they needed it to make a fish soup called Luk a mene. Marie ate many other traditional foods when she was growing up. Her family used

deer meat (venison) and even eel for some traditional recipes. Picking huckleberries and digging for edible roots in the woods was great fun, too. Marie used cedar baskets to carry the roots and berries home. The baskets were woven from cedar pieces that peeled off the trees like cornhusks. Her grandmother showed her how it was done.

Marie always went to nearby elementary schools, but when it was time to go to high school, she went away to a boarding school near Salem, Oregon, called Chemawa High School. She graduated in 1946. That was the same year she met Hadley Shilow. He had just come back from the war (World War II), and had been a prisoner of war for almost nine months. After Mr. Shilow got back, he found a job as a forest worker for the Yakama Indian Reservation and also for the Bureau of Indian Affairs (BIA). Marie and Hadley got married on October 20, 1947. During the first few years of their marriage, thry went on camping trips to Celilo Falls when there were still a lot of salmon to catch. But a dam was built on the river a few years later, and the falls disappeared. Now Mrs. Shilow can visit the falls only through pictures that were taken many years ago. Because of the dam there aren't as many Columbian salmon now either. This makes her sad.

Mr. and Mrs. Shilow made their home on the Yakama Indian Reservation. They were married more than 33 years before Mr. Shilow died. During their long and happy marriage, they were blessed with five children. All of the Shilow children graduated from high school and went to college. Morey was the oldest son and served two different tours of duty during the Vietnam War. He died of a heart attack when he was in his forties. The three other children, including Desi (Frances' mom), still live on the Yakama Reservation. Clinton works on an irrigation project for the BIA, and Beatrice works as a secretary for the Yakama Nation. Lucinda runs a college bookstore in Lewiston, Idaho, where she lives. All of the Shilow kids are very happy with their lives.

THE YAKAMA NATION

"All of the land where we live and where our ancestors lived was created for the [Indian] people." This belief about the creation of the world has been passed on

YAKAMA NATION

"Indians' Winter Encampment," a mural in Toppenish, Washington

by the Yakama for hundreds of years. The Yakama have always lived on the western part of the great Columbia River plateau in what is now Washington state.

The first Yakama hunted deer, elk, antelope, buffalo, mountain sheep, and goats. They counted on fish, roots, and plants for their food, too. The land has always been very important to the Yakama. They will tell you, "The land doesn't belong to the Indian; the Indian belongs to the land."

During the winter, the Yakama stayed in their villages. For the rest of the year, they lived in smaller camps and traveled from place to place looking for food. As time went on, they ate mostly fish and wild plants. Sometimes they hunted with bows and arrows. The deer was the most important animal to the Yakama because it gave them hides and other important parts to use for tools.

The Yakama were known for their expert basket making. Baskets were used to carry roots and store food. Human or animal figures decorated these baskets. Some of the

coiled baskets were used for cooking. To boil water in a basket, they dropped very hot rocks into the water that filled the basket.

The first Yakama houses were pit houses. They would dig a pit three to four feet deep. Over the pit they built a frame made out of poles and covered with mats of grass. On top of the grass mats they spread dirt. A hole in the roof let smoke out. This was also the door.

Over the years, the Yakama changed the kind of houses they lived in. They began to build houses with four walls called kaatnams. Building kaatnams started after they got horses. It was the horses that helped them move around more easily. All kaatnams had wooden frames. Two walls leaned toward each other and met at the top with poles. The other two walls were the ends. Tightly woven mats covered the walls, and poles were laid over the mats to keep them in place.

In Yakama tradition there are strong beliefs about what is right and wrong. Everyone followed these strict laws. If there was a problem, the chief acted as a judge. He had many other responsibilities besides being the leader. He had to help the needy during hard times and see that everyone followed the Yakama laws. The next most important people after the chiefs were the sub-chiefs. The sub-chiefs had special talents for hunting and fishing.

The Yakama had special people who were trained in medicine. They were called twakee, and they cured spiritual sicknesses. The medicine women were good at curing sicknesses, like colds or toothaches, with roots and plants. Medicine men and women were also asked to help the weather change, tell the future, and find lost objects.

Many special Yakama traditions are still kept today. You can find out more about Yakama at the Yakama Cultural Heritage Center. It has a museum, library, restaurant, school, R.V. park, and the Yakama Nation Sports Complex. At the Yakama Nation R.V. park, you can even rent a tipi for an overnight stay or two. All this is located in Toppenish, Washington.

CUSTOMS AND TRADITIONS

Traditional Names

Someday the children in the Smiscon family will have two names. Names are passed on to young family members to honor older relatives who have died. Children get their second name many years after they are born. This gives the family time to decide the best name to give them.

Mrs. Desi Smiscon and her two brothers and two sisters all have Native American names. Mrs. Smiscon was named I Yuff after her grandfather's mother. She got her name at her great-grandmother's funeral when she was four years old.

HISTORY TIMELINE

1700s In the early 1700s other Indian tribes brought horses to the Yakama, and they became good horsemen.

1775 The Continental Congress, which was working to form the new government for the U.S., said it was in control of Indians.

1805 The Yakama met Lewis and Clark, explorers for the U.S. government, on their trip to the Pacific Ocean.

1824 The Bureau of Indian Affairs was started to help Native Americans.

1825 The British and Yakama started trading for guns, gunpowder, tobacco, blankets, beads, and metal goods.

1850 Congress made a law called the Donation Act that let anyone settle on Indian land in the Pacific Northwest.

1855 The Treaty of 1855, between the United States and the fourteen bands and tribes of the Yakama Indian Nation, was signed. This was the beginning of the Yakama Nation government. This treaty said that Yakama reservation land was owned by all Yakama and open to all members of these tribes.

1855-58 The Yakama Nation and the U.S. went to war over the takeover of Indian land.

1859 The Yakama Treaty was approved and opened Yakama land to white settlers. The fourteen tribes of the Yakama Nation were moved onto reservation land.

1889 Washington Territory became a state.

1891 Reservation land was broken into small pieces and given to Yakama people. This was called the Allotment Act.

1914 Allotment on the Yakama Reservation ended.

1922 The Yakama Indian Agency moved from Fort Simcoe to Toppenish.

1924 Congress passed an act making Native Americans citizens of the United States.

1933 The Yakama people started their own government.

1934 The Yakama created their own constitution (rules to run government).

1935 The first Yakama Tribal Council met to restore self-government.

1946 The Enrollment Act passed. This meant that people who were at least one-fourth Native American from any of the fourteen tribes in that area could become members of the Yakama Nation.

1950s The Yakama Nation was paid more than $15 million by the U.S. government for taking Celilo Falls.

1955 The Yakama had laws made to help them buy back reservation land from people who wanted to sell.

1972 Mount Adams and old Yakama lands were given back to the Yakama people.

1977 The Yakama Nation published a book

called *The Land of the Yakamas* to help future generations know what their treaty rights are.

1980 The Yakama Cultural Heritage Center opened in June. The center is used for meetings, banquets, and special tribal programs. It has a museum, restaurant, gift shop, R.V. park, sports complex, theater, and library.

1992 The Yakama Nation changed the spelling of its name from Yakima to the traditional spelling, Yakama.

1994 In July, there were 8,487 members of the Yakama Nation.

Funerals

Many Yakama funerals are held at the long-house, in the Shaker Church, or at home. Most families choose just one place for the funeral, but when Mrs. Smiscon's brother Morey died, his funeral was held in three different places. On the first night, there was a service for him at his grandparents' home close to where he grew up. The next night, the family had a service at the Shaker Church where he used to take his grandparents. The third night, they had a service for him at the longhouse where his mother Marie Shilow is a member. A Yakama church is called a longhouse. Here they had a special ceremony for Morey's funeral. Seven drummers stood in the front of the longhouse and beat their drums. Another man rang a bell while people at the funeral performed traditional ceremonial dances.

There is another custom that happens a little while after a death. Family members give gifts to the family member who was given the relative's name. Mrs. Smiscon received gifts in honor of her great-grandmother when she got her second name. This is the way the family honors the dead person.

Weddings

The tradition of giving gifts is carried on in other ways, too. If a couple has a traditional Yakama wedding, their parents meet and make the plans. Instead of a minister or a judge, the parents marry their children in the ceremony. One or two years after an Indian Marriage Ceremony, there is a party. Members of the bride's and groom's families get together for an Indian Wedding Trade. This is a happy time when gifts are given to the bride and groom and family members on both sides. Each member of the groom's family brings a gift for one person in the bride's family. The bride's family does the same.

For example, the groom's aunt gives a present to the bride's aunt, and the bride's aunt gives a present to the groom's aunt. This tradition helps keep the two families close and brings them together in friendship. Marie and Hadley Shilow had an Indian Wedding Ceremony and Indian Wedding Trade. Their oldest daughter Lucinda and her husband had a "regular" wedding and an Indian Wedding Trade. The other children had regular weddings.

Memorials

Like weddings, other Yakama traditions have changed a little over the years. Another way to honor family members who have died is to bring out their names. The Smiscon family did this by having a basketball tournament to remember Mrs. Smiscon's father and brother, and a softball tournament in honor of their niece Shannon Nason. Other families might honor their dead with a memorial service because it brings people together and helps them remember their family.

Language

The Yakama language is another important part of the customs carried on in many Yakama families. Although English is the main language used by Yakama families, the Smiscon family uses many words from the Yakama language. This chart shows what they call their grandparents in their own language:

father's father	*Pu-sha*
father's mother	*Ah-lah*
mother's mother	*Kuth-tha*
mother's father	*Til-lah*

Here is a little story about using these names. When Desi Smiscon was growing up, her brother Morey played on a basketball team. She remembered his telling her a story about their Pu-sha. Pu-sha used to go and watch the basketball games. When the other children heard Morey holler, "Hi, Pu-sha," some of them thought this was his name and called him Pu-sha, too. These

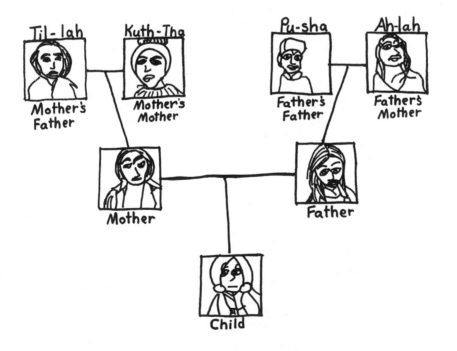

non-Native American kids didn't know that Pu-sha means grandfather. Pu-sha thought it was funny for so many children to be calling him grandfather. He laughed and said he would never be lonely with that many grandchildren.

Murals

Traditions of the past are often part of today's society. On the Yakama Reservation in Toppenish, Washington, beautiful murals depicting the past have been painted all over the town. One of the neat parts about the murals is that people from all different races worked together on the mural project. The whole community raised money to have them painted on walls of stores and other places where there was room. The murals tell the history of the Yakama Indians, the first settlers, and the soldiers of the United States government.

Mrs. Shilow, who has lived in this community most of her life, loves to see the history of her town. When she drives by the big mural of Celilo Falls, it brings back memories of when she and her husband were young and used to go salmon fishing. So if you go to Washington, remember to visit Toppenish and see the colorful murals painted on the walls and buildings of this town.

STORIES AND LEGENDS

Legends are stories that are passed down from generation to generation. These stories are very important because they give lessons about good and bad and tell how things came to be the way they are now. We have retold three Yakama stories for you.

"The Coyote and the Bear" will teach you about not being greedy. "The Star People" will tell you why there are stars in the sky, and "Chipmunk and the Old Witch" (At-at-a-tia) will teach you about obeying your parents. We hope you will learn from these Yakama stories like we did.

Coyote and the Bear

One day Coyote went out to fish. He sat by a stream and soon caught a fish. Coyote thought the fish he caught was too small, so he decided to set the fish down and try to catch a bigger one.

Coyote waited patiently and along came a bigger fish. Even though the second fish

was bigger, Coyote was still not happy with the fish he caught. Coyote set the medium-size fish next to the smaller fish and waited and watched for an even bigger fish.

Meantime, while Coyote was waiting for a bigger fish, Hungry Bear saw the two fish on the grass. Quietly, Hungry Bear sneaked up behind Coyote and stole the two fish without Coyote even noticing.

Finally, a very large fish swam by and Coyote jumped on the fish and dragged it back to the bank. Coyote thought to himself, "I'm going to take this fish along with the other two to my family."

When Coyote turned around to get the other two fish, he saw that they were gone. Hungry Bear had already eaten them. Coyote felt sad and ran home as fast as he could with only the large fish. The moral of this story is: Don't be selfish and try to get the biggest and best of everything. Another way of stating the moral: If you hoard and don't share, you must keep watch, day and night, against thieves.

The Star People

The star people were little people who lived in the forests. If adults tried to get into their forests, they scared them off. Worse yet, the star people would chase little children, catch them, and eat them.

One day, the star people chased a little boy and girl through their forest. The frightened children climbed up to the top of a very big tree. Suddenly the tree began to sway back and forth. Soon it came crashing to the ground.

When the tree hit the ground, it shook so hard it caused the tiny star people to fly up into the sky where they have lived ever since. This is how stars got into the sky.

This legend says that when you walk through the forest at night and look up, the star people look down and spy on you.

The Old Witch (At-at-a-tia)

Today, when children do not listen to their parents they are reminded of the wicked witch, At-at-a-tia. When she was alive, she was big and tall. She could be found in forests, rivers, and streams and in the deep dark woods that she watched over. Children and adults were not allowed in these woods because they were sacred grounds, and At-at-a-tia had to protect them. If any little children came too close to her special area or didn't listen to their parents, she would eat them up. Sometimes At-at-a-tia would even put children into her huge pockets.

There are many stories about At-at-a-tia. This is one of them.

Chipmunk and the Old Witch, At-at-a-tia

Once, a long time ago, there was an Old Grandmother Squirrel and her grandson Chipmunk. Old Grandmother Squirrel loved Chipmunk very, very much. They lived all by themselves in a small village next to the Hood River. From there, they could see the small Hood River flow past them to join the huge Columbia River.

Because they lived alone it was not easy to find enough food, but most people were kind enough to help them out. Some would bring them salmon in the spring. Others would bring them venison in the fall. If he could, Beaver would bring them eel.

When old Grandmother Squirrel needed to set food away for the long, cold winter, she dried it so it would keep for a long time. Old Grandmother Squirrel taught Chipmunk to gather nuts and seeds, something he could do all by himself. But she reminded him always to stay close to home because the mean, old, nasty witch who lived in the woods not far from their house loved to eat little chipmunk children!

Little Chipmunk loved to play around. One day when he went to the hills to gather nuts and seeds, he went a little too far away from home. At-at-a-tia saw him and started to chase after him. Little Chipmunk ran as fast as he could, but she ran faster and kept getting closer and closer to him!

Little Chipmunk ran like the wind until he spotted a tree. Onto the tree trunk he jumped, and up the tree he climbed with the mean, old, nasty witch right behind him. She reached out to grab him, but instead of catching him, her terribly long, evil fingernails only scratched down his back.

Little Chipmunk was very scared, but he tried to be brave up there on the top of the tree. Because of his patience and swift thinking, At-at-a-tia finally gave up and left. Still scared, Chipmunk scrambled down the tree and ran straight home to Old Grandmother Squirrel as fast as his legs could carry him.

Even today you will see little chipmunks and their friends playing and having a good time gathering nuts and seeds for winter.

But since Little Chipmunk did not listen to Old Grandmother Squirrel's warning, chipmunks still have scratch marks on their backs from the fingernails of At-at-a-tia.

FOOD AND FUN

Yakama people still eat lots of the same foods their ancestors ate many years ago. Some of their favorite native foods made from elk, deer, eel and salmon are fixed in many different ways. The Yakama also like huckleberry pies, dried hazelnuts, and blueberries.

In spring, some Yakama gather wild camas root, onions, potatoes, and carrots. In fall, they pick huckleberries. Some still hunt for deer, elk, and game birds during certain seasons. Once the food is gathered, the Yakama have feasts to celebrate each of the many kinds of foods found during different seasons.

Here are some Yakama recipes and crafts we would like to share with you.

Luk a Mene

A popular way to eat salmon is to use it in a delicious soup called Luk a mene. Luk a mene is Mrs. Shilow's favorite Yakama food. Even if you are not used to eating salmon, we think that you might like this recipe.

You will need:
1 can salmon (14¾ oz.)
4 cups of boiling water
4 cups of cold water
1 cup flour
salt and pepper to taste
large saucepan
mixing bowl
spoon

How to make Luk a Mene:
1. Pour 4 cups of water into the large saucepan and put it on the stove. Turn the heat on high.
2. While you're waiting for the water to boil, take the cold water and slowly add it to the flour in the mixing bowl. Keep stirring with a spoon so it doesn't get lumpy.
3. When the water on the stove starts boiling, slowly add the flour and water mixture to it. Make sure you stir it the whole time.
4. Drain the juice from the salmon and break the meat into chunks.
5. Add the salmon to the pan of water on the stove.
6. Sprinkle with salt and pepper so that it tastes the way you like it. Eat and enjoy!

Rose's Strawberry Jam

Rose Hadley Jim was Mrs. Shilow's mother. This jam is named after her. Many Native Americans in the Washington area used to make jams and jellies from wild huckleberries, strawberries, and gooseberries. Now when they make jam or jelly, most of them buy their berries at a fruit stand or in a store.

Rose used any jars she could find for her jam. She washed the jars nice and clean and boiled them in a big pot for five minutes. The jars had to be very, very hot when she put in the strawberry jam. Afterwards, she sealed them with paraffin wax melted in a double boiler or in a small pan set inside of a larger pan of boiling water.

Now for the recipe!

You will need:
2 pints fresh strawberries
7 cups sugar
3 oz. bottled liquid fruit pectin
7 small jars
1 package paraffin

How to make Rose's Strawberry Jam:
1. Wash the strawberries and cut them into slices.
2. Put 4 cups berries into a large saucepan and mix with one cup sugar. Make sure you mix the sugar and strawberries carefully. Leave this mixture alone for 15 minutes.
3. Put in the rest of the sugar and mix again.
4. Put the pan on the stove and bring the strawberry stuff to a full rolling boil. Let it boil hard for one minute. Keep stirring it, so it doesn't burn on the bottom of the pan.
5. Take the pan off the heat and stir in the pectin. Stir for five minutes more.
6. Scoop off the top layer of pink foam. Put the foam into a little bowl. It's really good when you eat it right away.
7. Spoon the jam into the very hot jars and pour the wax on top. This recipe makes 7 half-pint jars. It's wonderful to eat with fry bread!

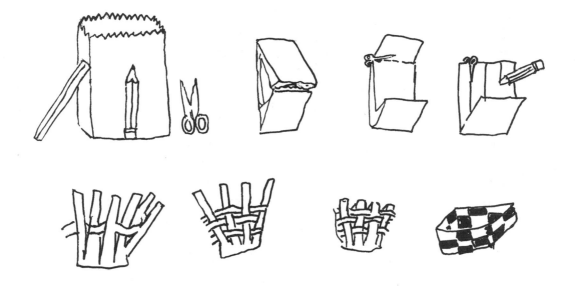

Baskets

Today, Yakama baskets are used mostly for decoration, but it is important to Mrs. Shilow to keep up the traditional craft of basketmaking in her family. Mrs. Shilow learned to make baskets by watching others. When she has spare time, she weaves baskets for her grandchildren. Many years ago when her grandmother made baskets, she used cedar and traded for the rest of the materials.

But today, Mrs. Shilow buys the long grass and basket materials at craft stores. She weaves the blades of grass back and forth to form the basket. If she sees a design or pattern she likes, she weaves it in. When she wants colorful designs in her basket, she dyes some of the grass. She hopes one day to teach her grandchildren how to make baskets.

Our class practiced the weaving process using paper bags and construction paper. We enjoyed this project and thought you would like to know how we made our paper baskets.

You will need:
paper lunch bags
construction paper strips, 1 inch thick by
    12 inches to 15 inches long (strips need
    to be long enough to go around the out-
    side of the bag)
scissors
pencil
ruler
tape or glue (tape seems to work better)
yarn or string (optional)

How to make a paper basket:

1. Take a folded lunch bag, fold it over one-third from the top, and crease it. Check to see if this is how high you want your basket to stand. You might need to cut some off the top.

2. Use a pencil and ruler to draw lines up and down your bag. Make sure there are an even number of lines, or it will be difficult to weave. Remember, the more lines you make the harder it will be to weave. Now, cut the along the lines but stop when you get to the bottom of the bag.

3. Take a strip of construction paper and tape it inside the bottom of the bag where you want to start weaving.

4. Carefully weave the paper over and then under the cuts in the bag. Tape the strip of construction paper to the bag each time it goes inside the bag.

5. After you have gone all the way around the bag with that strip, tape the end of it to the inside of the bag and cut off any extra with your scissors.

6. With another strip of construction paper, weave the opposite way. Go under where you went over, and over where you went under.

7. Repeat steps four, five, and six until you have one or two inches of the bag left at the top.

8. Carefully fold the tops of the bag down toward the inside. Tape each piece to hold it in place.

9. You may make a handle by taping a strip of paper, yarn, or string to either side of your bag.

Dream Catchers

There are many different traditions that are passed on about dream catchers. Frances Smiscon likes to hang them by her bed so they will catch her bad dreams and let her good dreams slip through. Then when the sun comes up, it kills the trapped ones. Frances made dream catchers for her mom and her grandmother to use in their cars as good luck decorations, and to help the good spirits watch over them when they drive on the highway. Remember, there are many ways to make dream catchers, but this is the way Frances makes them.

You will need:
leather (¼-inch-wide strips)
embroidery thread or waxed thread
a round hoop the size you want your dream
   catcher to be
beads, feathers, and other decorations
glue
toothpicks
scissors

How to make a dream catcher:

1. Wrap the leather around the hoop. Use glue if you have trouble making it tight, but use a toothpick to put the glue on, so you don't make it messy with too much.

2. Tie the string to the hoop. Start putting thread around the hoop to make your design. Frances loops it around the hoop only once, but we did it twice so we could keep it tight. Don't pull too tight or you will break the thread.

3. If you want, you can put a bead on while you are wrapping the thread.

4. Keep working your way to the center of the dream catcher. It will look sort of like a spider web.

5. After you are done, you can hang feathers from the bottom. We hung some beads on ours with an extra piece of leather and stuck the feather into the hole of the bead.

There are lots of books with ideas about how to make dream catchers. If you get good, you could even make earrings and other jewelry. Have fun!

OUR VISION FOR A BETTER TOMORROW

We hope that you have learned a lot about Yakama people. Some people think we still live in tipis, eat fish and berries, and ride wild horses. Even though we do some of these things on special occasions, we are just like other people. We feel like we're all just one small world made up of many cultures.

We are glad that the Smiscons have shared their family story and its Yakama traditions with us. Just like the Smiscons, we are working to keep our traditions alive, too. As students at the Yakama Tribal School, we wear jeans, sweats, socks, and tennis shoes like other kids. On special occasions like worship services, wedding trades, food gatherings, funerals, memorials, name-givings, and pow-wows, we are proud to wear our traditional Yakama clothing. Women and girls wear buckskin, jingle, wing, or cloth shell-trade dresses. Men and boys wear traditional Yakama grass dance outfits, ribbon shirts, beaded or Pendleton vests, and moccasins.

We still do many special Yakama traditions. We still live on some of the same land that has been part of our traditional culture for thousands of years.

Those of us who live on the reservation can see Mount Adams, a sacred mountain we call Pahto. The great mountain reminds us of the past and lifts our spirits. Pahto stands as a proud and beautiful symbol for the courage of our people today. We are a wonderful mixture of native Yakama and modern American culture and tradition. We are proud to be Yakama. We would like to be remembered as all-American and as traditional, native Yakama kids.

Mount Adams, the sacred mountain the Yakama call Pahto

EXPLORING THE SIOUX HERITAGE WITH CALVIN STANDING BEAR

Mr. Standing Bear teaches kids about his race.
When he plays his flute with a lot of grace,
You can see pride and respect on his face.
He helps make the world a better place.

Come with us and explore the life of the Standing Bear family. In this chapter, we will tell you the story of a family who is Lakota Rosebud Sioux. You will find out about their famous ancestors, about the Standing Bear's family heritage, and about their own family. You will even find out what the five Standing Bear children are like and what they like to do every day. They all helped us to write this chapter. Remember, all of this chapter is written from the stories that the Standing Bear family shared with us about their family's life.

CALVIN STANDING BEAR'S STORY

The first time we saw Calvin Standing Bear, he was on stage in Arvada, Colorado, performing in a musical play. He was an amazing sight. He stood out from everything else on the stage in his wonderful outfit of leather and beads. Fringe laced his sleeves and his shirt. Beads covered the front of his outfit, and his leather pants were fringed down the sides. His headdress was fantastic! It had feathers on top and down the back. His hair fell in two long braids and in front of his shoulders. When Calvin Standing Bear began to play his flute, the air was filled with a peaceful, expressive sound. The music caught our attention and seemed to tell a story about nature. It made us feel like we were flying through the air or watching a bird glide across the sky.

Mr. Standing Bear grew up near Denver, Colorado. Although he lived in a city, his family practiced many traditions connected to their heritage. Mr. Standing Bear still plays and sings Native American songs today. He

Olan Mills

Calvin Standing Bear in traditional dress

or three hours every day, he practices his music. He plays what he hears and makes his flute show the respect he feels. His flute sings to the water spirit, the water that brings us life. It tells us that the water here on earth is sacred.

Calvin Standing Bear's friend James Torres, a Chiracahua Apache, plays the keyboard and sings spiritual songs with him. The name of their musical group is the Red Tail Chasing Hawks. They make copies of their music for tapes and CDs. One CD on Canyon Records is called *Eagle Dances with the Wind*. Calvin and James sold some of their tapes after the performance we saw at the Cultural Arts Center, so we bought one. We have listened to our tape at least nine times and think the music is great. Calvin's music shares the Lakota Sioux heritage with others. He rewrites many traditional songs and plays them on guitar, drum and flute. He gives a new life to the music his people have enjoyed for so long.

One of the songs in Mr. Standing Bear's program is a very old one called the "Four Directions Song" that has been passed on from generation to generation. It tells the story of part of life's journey. Calvin Standing Bear asked us to stand when he sang this song because it is a sacred song, almost like a prayer. First, he sang to the west because the Thunderbeing comes from that direction. The Lakota Sioux believe that the Thunderbeing makes rain, snow, and sleet come from the sky. Next, he sang to the north because this is where the wind blows from. Then, he turned east and sang here because this is where we get our light.

knows how to play the guitar, the drums, and the flute. Even when he was young he liked music. As a little boy, he sang in Saint John's Cathedral Choir. He danced at powwows, too. A powwow is a gathering of Native Americans to celebrate a special occasion, like a chief's birthday.

Mr. Calvin Standing Bear has a job many people dream about. He says that the Spirit led him to make the music of his people. He writes his own songs and practices them on his flute until he can play them beautifully. First, he hears the music in his head, then he composes it. This doesn't just happen, it takes a lot of work and time. Two

Finally, he sang to the south because this is where the Creator of the world is. He told us that when a soul dies, it goes to the south. Then it travels over the Milky Way to the north and returns to the west where the Creator makes a new life.

During the program, Mr. Standing Bear explained to us that Lakota means "allies" in the Sioux language. It refers to all Indians. He uses Rosebud because he is from the Rosebud Reservation in the South Dakota Sioux Nation. A reservation is a piece of land that Native Americans were forced to live on when the United States government took away their land. At one time there were actually nine different Sioux reservations. Today, the reservations are Rosebud, Pine Ridge, Standing Rock, Cheyenne River, Lower Brule, Crow Creek, and Sisseton, all in South Dakota. People of Sioux blood also like to name themselves after their reservations.

Mr. Standing Bear travels to schools and teaches kids about Native Americans and the Lakota Rosebud Sioux. He told us he wanted us to have a good education. He said he liked coming to talk to us. When he spoke at our school, his voice was very

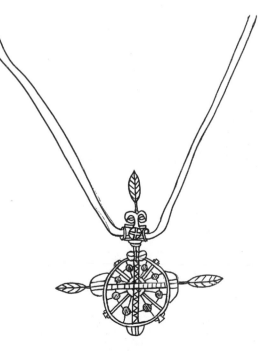

deep and quiet. He seemed peaceful and happy. He wore a necklace made of red, yellow, black, and white, the four traditional colors of the Lakota Sioux. Each color has special meaning. Red represents birth, health, and control. Yellow means thanksgiving, wisdom, and understanding. Black stands for pure water and thunder, and white stands for destiny and the renewal of life.

Mr. Standing Bear likes to tell kids how Native Americans are today. His own children go to school, play sports, and dress the same way their friends and classmates do. But they go to powwows, too, where they sing and dance the traditional dances. He wants his kids to learn about their Native American heritage.

Mr. Standing Bear feels that most cowboy and Indian movies don't show real Native American history and what made the lives of Indians so difficult. He believes these movies aren't very truthful because they show Indians as the bad guys. If kids don't understand Native Americans, it's because they see Indians always lose to cowboys in cartoons and western movies. Once when Calvin's grandfather

Luther Standing Bear was asked by the movie people to make a cowboy and Indian movie, he said, "No way! I will not be disrespectful to all Native Americans. This kind of stuff puts all Native Americans down."

THE FAMILY

Calvin Standing Bear's wife Irene is a full-blooded Navajo. She was raised on the Navajo reservation in Arizona, near a place called Skeleton Mesa. Mrs. Standing Bear has three brothers and four sisters. She speaks Navajo and has taught her children some of the Navajo language. Because the Standing Bear family is both Lakota Sioux and Navajo, Irene and Calvin Standing Bear are teaching their children the heritage of both nations. Mrs. Standing Bear has a big job taking care of her five children and helping them to become good citizens.

We enjoyed meeting the five Standing Bear children. At first, some of us who

Ron Horn

The Standing Bear family, clockwise from upper left: Rhonda, Luther, Antonia, Calvin Jr., Kimberly, Irene, and Calvin

weren't Native American thought they would be a lot different from us, but we found out they really weren't. As we sat together talking on our first day, we discovered that we are alike in many ways. Some of our favorite things to eat are Mexican, Chinese, and Italian food. We all enjoy playing sports and watching famous sports teams. In fact, all the Standing Bear children take tae kwon do lessons!

But there are a few things that make us different from each other. Those of us who aren't Native American had never been to a powwow before, or had never been given a special meaning for our names. Some of us had never done any type of beadwork either. These are some of the things that the Standing Bear children shared with us during their visit.

Seven-year-old Kim is the youngest Standing Bear. She says she likes first grade and her favorite subject is writing. At home, she likes helping her mother make fry bread. Sometimes her mother lets her make little tiny fry breads for herself. We will share their fry bread recipe with you later in the chapter, so we hope you're hungry!

Calvin Standing Bear Jr. is nine years old and in third grade. He told us how he really enjoys his tae kwan do lessons after school. His favorite movie is *Dragon, the Bruce Lee Story*. When he grows up he wants to be like his dad and play guitar and drum.

Rhonda is ten years old and in fourth grade. She really likes to visit her cousins on the Navajo reservation in Arizona. They always have a great time and like to have water fights.

Twelve-year-old Luther Standing Bear, a sixth-grader, told us how he got his special name.

"I like my name because I'm named after my grandfather Luther Standing Bear who was a Sioux chief. When he died, my grandma and my parents gave me his name. My Grandpa wrote four books: *My People the Sioux, Stories of the Sioux, Land of the Spotted Eagle*, and *My Indian Boyhood*. I feel very special when I read his books, because it's just like they were written for me. Sometimes I wonder if I will be famous like my grandfather when I grow up. I have thought about being an author, too, but I would also like to work in construction, building houses and other things."

Antonia Standing Bear is the oldest child in the family. She is 13 years old and a seventh-grader at Arvada Middle School. She shared some neat things that she likes to do. She taught us how to make pretty jewelry like earrings, necklaces, and bracelets. She told us that she likes making jewelry to give as gifts to her friends. Some of Antonia's teachers liked her jewelry so much that they even asked her to make some specially for them. We will show you how to make an awesome keychain in the Food and Fun section, so you can try it, too.

The four youngest Standing Bear children go to Lawrence Elementary School. The school year has many days that are used just for activities that help the students learn about different cultures. The students invite their parents to join them in classes and share their heritage with others. The Standing Bear family is always proud and happy to share their culture.

The Standing Bear Family's Personal Statement

We hope that everyone, especially children, learn to love and respect all people. We hope all Native Americans hold on to the special traditions of their nation, so they can share them with their children and others. Our country will be strong if we keep the best of all different heritages and remember to practice those customs and traditions in our lives.

THE SIOUX NATION

The Sioux once lived in the area that is now Minnesota. About 300 years ago they moved, mostly by walking, to the Great Plains. They had dogs that carried some of their things, but they had to carry most of their belongings on their backs.

Somewhere along the way, they found wild horses and learned how to ride them. Then they could travel and hunt buffalo a lot easier. By the time they got to the Great Plains, they were excellent horseback riders and buffalo hunters.

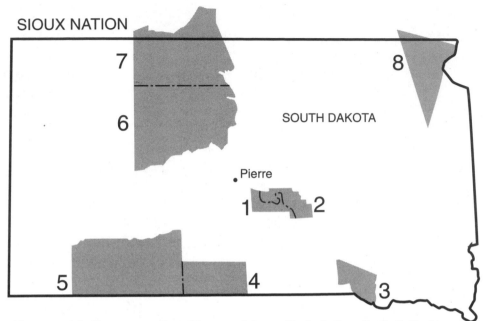

SIOUX NATION

SOUTH DAKOTA

Pierre

There are eight Sioux reservations. They are: 1. Lower Brule, 2. Crow Creek, 3. Yankton, 4. Rosebud, 5. Pine Ridge, 6. Cheyenne River, 7. Standing Rock, and 8. Sisseton.

The Sioux nation was so large that it was broken into seven groups called the Seven Council Fires. Each group had its own leaders and its own families who always camped together. The Seven Council Fires lived in an area that went from what is now Minnesota to Montana and from Wyoming to Nebraska. The seven groups did not always speak the same dialect, but they would all get together sometimes to trade and share news. At these big gatherings it was the custom to take part in the Sun Dance. The Sun Dance honored their promise to give thanks to the Great Spirit for the past year and to ask for help for the new year.

The Sioux lived in tipis made out of poles and buffalo hide. Tipis were light and easy to move. They were waterproof and strong against the wind. They were always warm in the winter and cool in the summer.

The Sioux never camped in one place for very long. They followed buffalo herds and moved about so their horses could always find fresh grass. Horses were very important to the Sioux. A family was rich if they had a lot of horses. Different tribes would often raid each other to steal horses.

The Sioux needed buffalo to survive. They used every part of the buffalo; nothing was wasted. Because they believed the buffalo was a holy animal, they would say special prayers before killing one.

When the men returned from a successful buffalo hunt, those who had stayed behind cheered the hunters. The women

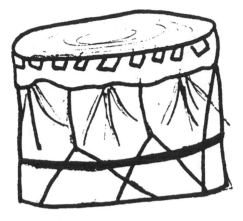

boiled or roasted the fresh meat over camp-fires, and the whole group celebrated with a big feast. Everyone danced to the beat of a drum. Extra meat was cut into strips and smoked over the fire or dried in the sun so it could be saved for later. The buffalo skins were cleaned, dried, and softened and later made into clothes, shoes, and storage bags. Many skins were sewn together for tipis.

Girls were taught by their grandmothers to cook and sew. They learned how to prepare buffalo skins and how to put up tipis. Boys were taught by the men to hunt for the food their families would need.

Prayer was important in the life of the Sioux. They believed the Great Spirit had power over all things. They would pray and sing songs to the Great Spirit. Only a few people in each tribe were trained to be doctors. They were called medicine men and women. They knew exactly which plants could be used to cure colds, or toothaches, or even broken bones.

Everything the Sioux made had beautiful designs and colors. They painted their tipis, their robes, and their shields. These paintings told stories about brave deeds that had been done or about special dreams they had been given. Designs were made by the women with porcupine quills, beads, shells, and eagle feathers. Each tribe had its own special design. The Sioux did not write their language down. Instead, they made pictographs with symbols and pictures that told stories about the tribe's history. These paintings were done only by the men. They would paint symbols on rawhide to show all the important events that happened in their tribe.

Storytelling was important to the Sioux because this was how they remembered their history. Summers were busy with hunting and gathering food, so storytelling happened only in the winter when the tribe

HISTORY TIMELINE

1600s The Sioux moved west from the area that is now Minnesota when European fur traders settled on their land.

1700s The Sioux caught wild horses to help them hunt buffalo. Horses become very important to the Sioux.

1850s When the railroad was built across the country, white "sportsmen" killed buffalo for sport or just for their hides. The meat was left to rot on the plains.

1868 The Fort Laramie Treaty was signed. This treaty made the Indians give up a lot of land but promised them that no white settlers or gold seekers would be allowed on the land they still had left.

1876 A deadline was set by the U.S. government. All Indians had to be living on a reservation by January. Indians not living on a reservation would be thought of as dangerous and could be killed. The Sioux and the Cheyenne got together to protect their people.

1876 In June, the two nations attacked U.S. troops and moved on to camp by the Little Big Horn River.

1876 In late June, General George Custer and his troops attacked the two tribes who were camped by the river. This was called the Battle of the Little Big Horn, the Sioux's biggest victory. The Indians were led by Sitting Bull and Crazy Horse. Custer and all of his men were killed. Even though the Sioux won, they were forced back to the reservation.

1885 Many of the buffalo that roamed the plains were killed. Government force and lack of food drove the Indians back to the reservations again.

1890 U.S. troops were sent to stop the Ghost Dance. They were afraid the Sioux would start fighting with them again. When Sitting Bull was killed by U.S. soldiers, Chief Big Foot's tribe panicked. They tried to get away from their reservation to a place called Wounded Knee, but the soldiers followed and killed 200 to 300 Sioux men, women, and children. This is known as the Massacre at Wounded Knee.

1944 The National Congress of American Indians was formed to help make laws to protect Native Americans.

1973 An argument broke out over tribal leadership on the Pine Ridge Reservation. A group of about 200 Native Americans took over the village of Wounded Knee, South Dakota, for 71 days. Two people were killed and more than 300 arrested.

1980 The U.S. Supreme Court ordered the federal government to pay more than $100 million to the Sioux for taking the Black Hills in 1877.

had plenty of time to relax. Storytelling was a way for the old people to share their memories and the lessons they had learned with the young ones.

Like other tribes, the Sioux had to fight to keep their land. The Sioux believed land should be shared and not owned, but the white settlers wanted to own their land. Sometimes the U.S. troops attacked the Sioux, and sometimes the Sioux attacked the troops. Sadly, there were many famous battles like Little Big Horn between them. After the last battle, the Sioux were forced to live on reservations. There were no buffalo to hunt on reservations, so the Sioux had to learn how to live in a new way.

Today, the Sioux live a more modern life. Some live on reservations, while others have moved away. Many Sioux keep traditions going in their families. They do not use horses to travel anymore. Horses are used for rodeos and sports. Traditional dancing and singing are very important to the Sioux. The Sun Dance is still danced, and traditional prayers are still offered. Gatherings called powwows now bring different tribes together from all over the United States and Canada.

CUSTOMS AND TRADITIONS

Respecting Elders

A very important part of the Sioux tradition is respect for elders. As an elder herself, Ms. Neva Standing Bear, Calvin's mother, has taught her children and grandchildren to honor all living things. Because the Standing Bear family respects their grandmother and what she has taught them, we want to share what we learned from her about their spiritual beliefs.

Neva Standing Bear told us how she became a spiritual leader for her people. Spiritual leaders are members of the tribe who help people with their spiritual needs. One day, Ms. Standing Bear opened her front door to find two men standing there. They were spiritual leaders from her tribe. They asked if she had a pipe. Many times a pipe is smoked when important things are talked about. The tradition of Neva Standing Bear's people is that you agree to do whatever someone asks when you smoke the pipe together. The spiritual leaders asked Ms. Standing Bear to become a spiritual leader. Her answer was yes.

Becoming a spiritual leader was a great honor for Neva Standing Bear, and she is thankful to have this important responsibility. Now she gives blessings and prays for sick people. When people ask for her prayers, she prays from the heart. People often come to her for advice, too. Officials of the new Denver International Airport invited her and her son Calvin Standing Bear to come lead a prayer and give a blessing for a safe airport. Many people believe the airport land used to be a burial place for Native Americans. But Neva Standing Bear reminded us that part of her Sioux and Christian heritage is to give prayers of thanks when good things like the new airport happen.

Drumming and Dancing

Drumming is another important part of Sioux life. Emilio Casica told us how he feels about drumming. He said the drum shows us the circle of life. This is why he feels it's important for all Native Americans to know how to drum. Two of our authors belong to drum groups. They drum, sing, and dance at different powwows. They taught us how to listen for the four basic beats they use when they play. With each different dance they do, the beat changes.

Another big part of Native American heritage is dancing. Many of our authors have kept this tradition alive. The dancing is done to the music of the drum. Men do the drumming on small round drums or in a group sitting around a big drum. Even

Author Emilio Cosica performs for the other writers

Ron Horn

young boys are encouraged to take part. Over the years, many of the dances from each nation have been shared and blended together.

Traditional dance is like a soaring eagle. It is the slowest of all the dances because the drum plays a slow beat. On the traditional dance outfit, bustles made of eagle feathers are tied on in back and on each arm. It looks almost like the dancers have wings. Dancers wear ribbon shirts and ribbon cuffs. Traditional dancers also wear buckskin moccasins and breast plates made out of bone and beads. As a sign of respect, women and girl dancers wear a traditional fancy shawl to cover their backs.

Fancy Dance is the hardest of the dances. It is fast and fun. It takes a long time to learn because it has lots of quick body motion with splits and flips. That's why it's called Fancy Dance! You need lots of coordination and strong legs to do this dance. The Fancy Dancer wears a headdress, and the Fancy Dance outfit is covered with beads and horsehair, too. Two bustles hang on the back and one on each arm.

The third dance is the Grass Dance. It is like the swaying movements of the tall grass on the prairie, waving in the breeze. This dress has lots of fringe made out of yarn. As the dancer moves, the fringe sways like grass in the wind. We watched one of our authors, John Thomas, do a Grass Dance. It looked very hard.

When we talked with the dancers, they told us that the outfits they wear are very special. They are a part of the dance. We learned that touching an eagle feather or

Ron Horn

Author John Thomas does a grass dance

a plume on a dancer's dress is disrespectful. The dress is made to be a piece of art. Dancers must earn the honor to wear the traditional dress when they dance.

Some of our Native American authors taught the rest of us how to do the Friendship Dance. For some of us it was the first Native American dance we had ever done. It made us feel much closer in friendship to our new Native American friends.

STORIES AND LEGENDS

There are many stories that are passed on from generation to generation in the Native American heritage. Many of these are retold by an elder of the family or can be found in library books. One of our favorite parts of Mr. Standing Bear's visit was listening to his stories. A special Lakota Sioux story passed on in the Standing Bear family comes from their grandfather Luther Standing Bear. We liked "Standing Bear's Horse" the very best, so we chose to retell this story for you!

Standing Bear's Horse

For many years, the enemies of the Sioux had been troubling them, taking their horses, and killing the buffalo. After a while, the warrior Standing Bear the First asked the braves to go with him to punish their enemies. Ten warriors said they would go and help, and soon they all set out to find their enemies. All except Standing Bear traveled on foot. He rode his beautiful horse, one of his most prized possessions. For days they traveled toward the boundary of their land, but the enemies kept out of sight, because they knew the Sioux were very brave fighters.

Now, between the warriors and their tipis on the bank of Porcupine Creek, lay the Great Plains. The warriors journeyed over these beautiful plains with their soft waving grasses. Animals were feeding everywhere. Many days passed.

When at last the Sioux found their enemies, they gave them punishment for what they had done. Once that was over, the warriors were glad to turn their backs and go home again.

As the Sioux were returning to their homes, they were shocked to find that an awful fire had swept their land. Black, scarred plains stretched on as far as the eye could see. As the days went by, the food the warriors had brought along ran out. The Sioux warriors were hungry and looked everywhere for food, but all the animals had run away to escape the fire. Even Standing Bear's horse could find nothing but a few clumps of grass to eat. The warriors traveled for days and they saw no buffalo or any other animals.

At night when the warriors slept, Standing Bear's faithful horse stood guard. He woke them if he saw something strange. He seemed to know the warriors were too weak and tired to watch. Finally, the day came when the warriors said to Standing Bear, "We can't go on. You must kill your horse so we can survive." Standing Bear was brokenhearted. He didn't want to kill his best friend, his faithful horse. With great sadness, Standing Bear turned to the warriors and said, "Wait for another day to come. If tomorrow we cannot find any food, I will kill my horse to save our lives." Standing Bear turned again and said, "I will take my horse and go and pray to the Great Mystery for food."

Slowly, he rode to the top of a hill. There, Standing Bear closed his eyes and prayed for food so that the warriors and his horse would be saved. When he opened his eyes again, a miracle had happened. Below the hill stood a buffalo grazing in a patch of green grass near a spring. Standing Bear and his horse knew they had to catch that buffalo. The horse ran and ran and Standing Bear fired two shots. The first shot weakened the buffalo, and the second one killed it. Standing Bear knew his prayer had been answered. He began skinning the buffalo, so he could take food back to his warriors. Years later, Standing Bear showed his son the exact place he had prayed and found the buffalo.

If you would like to read some of the other stories written by Luther Standing Bear, you can find them in a book called *Stories of the Sioux*.

The Story of Creation

This creation story is not a Lakota Sioux story. It is a Native American story special to Mr. Standing Bear and his family. We have retold "The Story of Creation" in our own words, so you can enjoy it, too. Remember that this may be a little different from creation stories you might read in another book, but this is the way the story is told in the Standing Bear family.

Once there was a world before this one that didn't please the Creator. The Creator had been noticing how the humans were misbehaving and decided to make it rain until the whole world was flooded. Before he flooded the world, he placed his pipe into his pipe bag and hung it on the pipe rack. Soon, it started to rain and rain. After it rained and rained, the Creator sang a song and stomped on the ground. His stomping made big cracks, and water gushed furiously out of the cracks. It rained and rained some more. The Creator floated on his huge pipe bag and let the waves carry him along. At last the rain stopped, and there were no more people.

Only one living creature could be seen. It was a crow named Kange who flew over the Creator and the water. The bird told the Creator that he needed a resting place. Kange was so tired and hungry he asked the Creator three times for a resting place.

The Creator picked up his pipe bag, reached into it, and pulled out a loon, a diving bird. The Creator asked the diving bird to dive to the bottom of the water and bring back a lump of mud, so he could make land for Kange to rest on. The Creator sang a song to help the loon get down to the mud. The loon gladly obeyed the Creator's request and dove into the crystal clear water. He went so far his lungs ached. The loon returned to the surface and said, "I couldn't make it, I almost died." The Creator said it was okay and put him aside.

Then the Creator reached into his bag and pulled out an otter. The otter had strong, webbed feet to help him swim. The Creator told the otter he would sing a song so he could dive all the way to the mud. Now the sleek otter took a deep breath and dove down as far as he could go, but he never got to the bottom. His wet fur sagged as he told the Creator that he couldn't make it. The Creator said, "That's okay," and put him aside.

Next, the Creator reached into the bag and took out a beaver. The beaver had a strong, flat tail to help him go down. He told the same thing to the beaver. The beaver dove. And though he stayed under the water longer than the others, he also came up with nothing.

At last the Creator reached into his bag and pulled out the turtle. "You must bring the mud," the creator told the turtle. As the turtle dove into the water, the Creator sang a spiritual song for him. The turtle felt very special that the Creator had asked him to help. He kept swimming deeper and deeper because he knew he would make it. The Creator waited and waited. The animals started to cry, they were so worried. The crow continued to fly in circles, crying all the while that he had to have a place to rest. Finally, after a very long time, the turtle came back up, breathing as hard as he could. "I have the mud," he told the Creator, and the Creator took the mud.

The Creator sang as he made a circle out of the mud. When he stopped singing, there was enough land for both the Creator and the crow. Next, the Creator took an eagle feather out of his pipe bag and began waving it over the land. As he did this, he commanded the land to spread. Then he stopped and thought to himself, water without land is not good, but land without water is not good, either. The Creator began to cry in sorrow. He felt sorry for the creatures he was going to put on the land without water. His tears became lakes and rivers and oceans of salt water.

The Creator reached into his pipe bag and took out animals, birds, and plants and spread them all over the land. He then took the four colors of earth, red, white, black, and yellow, and made human beings. And this is why we have many colorful races today.

Irene and Antonia Standing Bear show the students how to make fry bread

FOOD AND FUN

In this section, we will share with you some favorite recipes and fun crafts and games.

Fry Bread

This is a favorite Native American food. The Navajo people eat fry bread, and so do the Sioux. We made it when Mrs. Irene Standing Bear came to our writing workshop. She is Navajo and grew up on a reservation in Arizona. When she was a little girl, she used to watch her mother just pour in the ingredients without measuring. That's how Mrs. Standing Bear learned how to make it without measuring. It was amazing that she knew just how much of each ingredient to put in. But since some of us hadn't watched our moms make it, we found a recipe with the same ingredients that Mrs. Standing Bear used. It is fun to make.

You will need:
4 cups flour
4 teaspoons baking powder
2 teaspoons salt
2 to 2½ cups water
½ cup powdered milk
2 to 3 cups of oil

How to make fry bread:
1. Take all the dry ingredients and mix them in a bowl with your hands until they are mixed well.
2. Pour a little water into the dry ingredients and mix well. Keep doing this until you have enough water to make it stick together. It may stick to your hands when you mix it, but that's okay. The dough should be well-mixed and smooth.
3. Put about a teaspoon of oil into another bowl and grease it by spreading the oil around with your hand. Leave the dough in the other bowl and let it sit there for awhile until it rises.

4. When the dough feels dry to your touch, pour some oil into a deep-fat fryer and heat it. Be sure that you have your mom or dad help you, since it is easy to get burned by the oil.

5. Take a section of the dough, about the size of a lemon, in your hand and flatten it out. Pinch a small hole in the center using your thumb and pointer finger. Gently put the dough into the oil so the oil does not splash. Be careful not to touch the hot oil. Remember, the bread won't sizzle if the oil is not hot enough. If you want to be sure the oil is hot enough, drop a piece of dough about the size of a quarter into it. When the dough sizzles and comes to the top, the oil is hot enough.

6. Turn the bread over with a fork when the bottom gets brown. As soon as both sides are done, put the fry bread into a bowl lined with paper towels to keep it warm.

7. Put honey, powdered sugar, jelly, or butter on the warm fry bread.

8. Eat and enjoy!

This was the best fried bread we'd ever had, and it smelled really good. It was chewy and a little like sopapillas, a Mexican fried bread served for dessert. You can have fry bread with your dinner or for dessert. Make it for company, for a holiday or birthday, for a special person, or just for yourself.

Wojapi

Once you make the fry bread, you may want to eat it with a special dip called *wojapi*. It is sort of like a pudding for special occasions like Christmas and birthdays.

Mr. Standing Bear told us wojapi is a spiritual food used in ceremonies, too.

The recipe below may not be the same for each Native American family. Each family will change the recipe to fit their preferences and their heritage. Just because a family uses a different recipe doesn't mean their recipe is wrong. For example, your mother may have a special recipe for fried chicken, but your best friend's mother may make it differently. So, does this mean that it is wrong? No! The fried chicken is made the way your family has made it over the years. It's the same with the wojapi recipe. It may be different, but it's not wrong.

You will need:
1 16½ oz. can blueberries
1 can water (½ can hot and ½ can cold)
¼ cup flour
2 tablespoons cornstarch
sugar (if you want to make it sweeter)

How to make wojapi:
1. Heat the blueberries with ½ can of hot water in a saucepan.
2. Smash blueberries in the pan as they heat up.
3. In a jar, mix flour, corn starch and ½ can cold water. Shake until it is a thin paste. (This keeps the soup from getting lumpy.)
4. When the berries boil, add the cornstarch/flour paste.
5. Taste and add sugar if you need to make it sweeter.
6. Stir until it is thick, then take the pan off of the stove.
7. The soup should be the texture of pie

filling. If it is too thin, add a little more paste made with flour, cornstarch, and water like you did before. If it is too thick, add a little more water. If you use it as a dip, be careful not to let it drip on you, because it is served hot and it might stain your clothes.

We hope you will try this recipe. One of our authors ate five bowls, he thought it was so wonderful! We recommend you eat only two, though, so you don't get sick. Ms. Standing Bear told us you can use any dark berries, but we liked blueberries best because they don't have seeds and are very sweet. You may want to try your favorite berries and come up with a special recipe of your own.

Key Chains

Antonia Standing Bear was taught to make key chains by her Aunt Roberta, who is Sioux. Antonia taught our class how to do it. If the directions seem hard, look at the pictures. They will help you follow the directions.

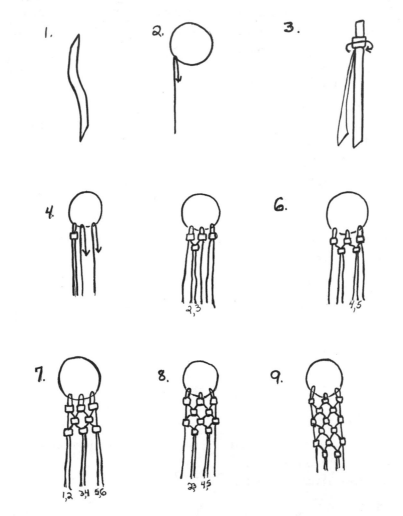

You will need:
1 key ring
three thin leather strips,
  about 18 inches long
12 to 30 ¼-inch plastic colored beads with large
  holes

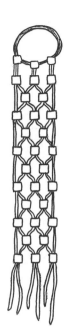

How to make a key chain:
1. Cut the ends of the leather strips so they're pointed.
2. Fold one strip of leather through the key ring.
3. Thread the two ends of the leather strip through one bead, and push the bead to the top. (Twisting helps.)
4. Fold the other two leather strips through the key ring and repeat step 3.
5. Take strips 2 & 3 and thread a bead to the top.
6. Take strips 4 & 5 and thread a bead to the top.
7. Go back and thread a bead on strip 1 & 2, 3 & 4, 5 & 6.
8. Thread beads on 2 & 3, 4 & 5.
9. Repeat the pattern, alternating:
a. 1 & 2, 3 & 4, 5 & 6
b. 2 & 3, 4 & 5

After you are done, you will have a beautiful key chain. It's fun to make, but it's hard to push the leather through the beads. It got easier as we went along. Some kids had theirs done in half an hour, and some took up to two hours. The chains were pretty, especially with the diamond shapes in the middle.

You can use the same idea to make a necklace, a leash, a pacifier holder, earrings, or decorations for your hair. You can make them for birthday or Christmas presents. A key chain is a great gift for someone who just got a driver's license. Or you could just make something for yourself.

Drums

The Standing Bear family also taught us how to make drums. Their drums probably looked a little better than ours, but we know you will enjoy doing this as much as we did.

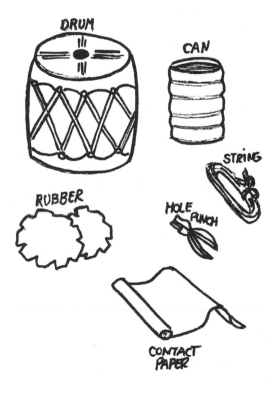

You will need:
a coffee can
can opener
2 pieces of rubber from an old inner tube (we got ours from a tire store in our neighborhood)
contact paper that looks like wood
leather strips about four arm's lengths long
scissors
hole punch
paint and/or markers

How to make a drum:
1. Cut both ends out of the coffee can using a can opener.
(Watch out for the sharp edges.)
2. Place the contact paper around the outside of the can.
3. Cut 2 round pieces of rubber about 1½ inches larger than the top of the can.
4. Cut little triangles, about ½ inch apart, around the edges of each rubber piece.
5. Punch holes in the tabs between the triangles.
6. Put the two pieces of rubber on either end of the can.
7. Thread the leather back and forth through the holes, starting at the top of the can and then going to the bottom.
8. Tie off the ends of the leather.
9. Decorate your drum with paint or markers, or leave it plain.
10. Practice playing different beats on your drum.

OUR VISION FOR A BETTER TOMORROW

We, the authors, felt so lucky to have met the Standing Bear family. They are wonderful people who are making a difference by helping others understand Native Americans both past and present. These are just a few of the things we learned.

If you are going to make fun of someone, you should first stop and think, "Would you like it if someone made fun of you?" Just think how you would feel if you were being teased.

Native Americans are alive today, not just in the past.

Don't expect people to know all about their own heritage. There is always more to learn about your culture and others.

Judge people by their heart, not their looks.

The neatest thing we learned is that people are the same in many ways. We hope you have come to see the ways the Sioux culture, your own culture, and other cultures are alike.

WESTRIDGE YOUNG WRITERS WORKSHOP PARTICIPANTS

Director: Judith H. Cozzens, Assistant Director: Robbin Kitashima

Each chapter was written by a different group of teachers and student authors. Here are their names.

MUSCOGEE (CREEK) CHAPTER PARTICIPANTS

Dustin Elementary School

Teachers
Carol Selvidge and Robin Fife

Authors
Chasity Billy
Tony Joe Brown
James Fife
Jacob Goodno
Alice Harjo
Kamie Horne
Aleasha Littlebird
Ruthanne McGirt
Joe Resendiz
Ryan Robertson

Henryetta Elementary School

Teachers
Madeline Duncan and Sandy Fife Wilson

Authors
Aaron Brennan
Katie Bryan
Kari Carender
Aaron Carley
Lindsay Goodman
Ryan Green
Joe Harrison
Stephen Hendricks
J. P. Knox
Sharry Mouss
Jeff Nunn
Sonja Ortman
Feanil Patel
Mrugesh Patel
Robert Sessions
Nicole Taylor

Linda Thomas

Westridge Elementary School

Teachers
Suzanne Swank and Cherylene Evans

Classroom Assistant
Staci Fife Patrick

Authors
Ann Abrahamson
Jason Burroughs
Vanessa Chandler
Megan Conti
Amanda Copenhaver
Breann Dillow
David J. Downey
Roseanne Gawne
Simone Hicks
Cassie Kendrick
Grace Kruszewski
Theresa McCullar
Geoffrey Morse
Brian J. Noble
Randy Reardon
Jacob Simpson
Kevin Sokoloski
Sarah Swetlic
Adam Thompson
Andrew Tope
Brandon Towner
Mary Ann Vuletich
Shane Wagner
Jessica Walls
Jessica Welch
Tara Zobjeck

ARAPAHO CHAPTER PARTICIPANTS

Arapaho School

Teacher
Mrs. M. Dabich

Ron Horn

Ms. Evans' and Ms. Swank's class—Muscogee chapter authors

Ruth Kelly

Mrs. Duncan's class—Muscogee chapter authors

Darlene H. Hallam

Mrs. Dabich's class—Arapaho chapter authors

Authors
Yolanda Antelope
Kristina Behan
Shawn Durgin
Colleen Friday
Susan Headley
Malena Johns
Aimee Kunst
Ebenezer Littlethunder
Krystal Miller
Darrell Moss, Jr.
Ivy Robertson
Jessica Whiteman
Alfred Willow
Annie Willow

Westridge Elementary School

Teacher
Ms. Cheryl Waits

Authors
Stephanie Bertucci
Kelley Bleyle
Tiffany Bott
Zachary A. Brown
Lance Colaiannia
Ben Dallet
Mike Davis
Chandra Emmons
Jason R. Fox
Scott Gustafson
Christina M. Hart
Darren Hazel
Jason Jumps
Michelle L. Keller
Jennifer Knutson
Alexis Cummins LeCoq
Emily C. Lienemann
Danielle Mariscal
Matthew McCabe
Natalie Medrano
Joseph Lee Ramos
Angie Recktenwald
Kevin Reilly
Joey Romeo
Tasha Ruybal
Stephanie Soos
Sean Walters

NAVAJO CHAPTER PARTICIPANTS

Window Rock Elementary School

Teachers
Isadore Begay, Marie Enfield, and Wanda Heronemus

Classroom Assistants
Irene Scott and Edison Scott

Isadore Begay's Class
Authors
Jason Jay Berchman
Jancita Cadman
Sheena Clark
Tessa Descheeny
Staci Etsitty
Aaron Haskie
Nicole Haven
Myron High Elk
Chris Hilt
Matilda Jordan
Loren Tooahvonie Lincoln
Kelly R. Manuelito
Antionette Nez
Nadine Gwen Notah
Nicole Spencer
Alisha V. Tsosie
Denise Tulley
Sean M. Yazzie
Shereen Yazzie
Solomon Yellowhorse

Marie Enfield's Class
Authors
Rana T. Begaye
Gabriel Betsoi
Jarrett Bia
Desi Rae Deschenie
Stanford Etsitty
Roxanna Rose Gruber
Travis Henson
Crystal Shea Ipalook
Eric Johnson
Michael King
Adrian Luarkie
Alvonna Lynch
Vita M. Roan
Erin Scott

Ms. Waits' class—Arapaho chapter authors

Mr. Begay's class—Navajo chapter authors

Mrs. Enfield's class—Navajo chapter authors

Eric Allan Shurley
Crystal Silver
Nina Marie Sloan
Terry Jay Tsosie
William Upshaw
Akeem Watson
Annastacia Yazzie
Darrell Yazzie

Mrs. Wanda Heronemus'
Class Authors
Angelo A. Ashley
Marvin Belone
Philmore Chee
Jules L. Claw
Jonah Damon
Orena Daniels
Jeremiah B. Deschine
Robert C. Flake
Arminda Desbah Foster
Kyle Harrison
Candice Kelwood
Jerom Prows
LaNell K. Shirley
Christopher B. Smelser
Danielle Lynn Smith
Brandon Torivio
Tiffany Tso
Crystal Lynn Tulley
Kimberly L. Williams

HOPI CHAPTER PARTICIPANTS

Teacher
Fred Salazar

Teacher's Assistant
Linda S. Salazar

Authors
Ryan A. Balderas
Dustin Bridges
Brian Allen Buzzard
Becky Carlson
Aileen Clark
Alicia E. Cody
Amanda Rosa Daniel
Cassidi C. Daniels
Ashlie Daulton
Marissa Delgarito
Jamie Lynn Doerr
Jim Dugan

Sarah Epperson
Lindsay Marie Gillis
Bradley W. Gruters
Laura Hartstone
Sherard Harvey
Quintin Hegedus
Chris L. Hicks
Natalie L. King
Cole Middlebrook
Sara E. Morley
Raven Murray
Travis Aaron Reiner
John Shimkus
Molly Mae Stone
Rebecca Wheeler
Chris Wills
Adam Wilson
Cameron Wyatt

YAKAMA CHAPTER PARTICIPANTS
Yakama Tribal School

Teacher
Deepika Adhikari Janke

Authors
Adelle Barney
Loni Davis
Rosanna Frank
Samantha Heemsah
Derek Robert Mayokok
Red Eagle Miller
Tamera Reyes
Johnny Sampson
Lona Shippentower
Martha Wahpat
Edwin Wheeler
Emery Yallup

Peiffer Elementary School

Teacher
Edith Glapion

Teachers Assistants
Karen Batchelder, Bryan
Brammer, and Lila Salazar

Authors
Matthew Dayne Beck
Jacilynn Brandon
Kirk Ryan Brister

Mrs. Heronemus' class—Navajo chapter authors

John Cozzens

Mr. Salazar's class—Hopi chapter authors

John Cozzens

Ms. Janke's class—Yakama chapter authors

Marian Stewart

Christian J. Charczuk
Amanda Clark
Harold "Chip" Doiron
Katherine Doyle
Daniel Feuerstein
Keenan M. Franklin
Brooke Ann Gitt
Breanne L. Hansen
Cody Lee
Scott P. Legler
Travis J. Martin
Jennifer Morgan
Timothy Petrucci
Stefanie Recktenwald
James R. Schanke
Josh Schoedel
Stacey K. Semm
Jessica Shilling
Darren Steinle
Rory Valley
Heather A. Williams

Tiko T. Lynch
Chelsea M. Lyons
Kelly MacCary
Natalie Moore
Ryan Nickersen
Eric T. Noble
Garrett Port
Monica D. Ruybal
Zach Smith
Antonia Standing Bear
Calvin Standing Bear
Kimberly Standing Bear
Luther Standing Bear
Rhonda Standing Bear
Malory Theis
John Thomas (Mad Bear)
Carlos Warclub
Maria Warclub
Lani Wiese

LAKOTA ROSEBUD SIOUX CHAPTER PARTICIPANTS

Teachers
Beth Herburger, Diana Kline, and Michelle Dimanna

Authors
Jennifer Allen
Tim Anderson
Tyler Anstett
Lars M. E. Barricklow
Emilio Few Feathers (Poblano) Casica
Melissa A. Chaudhuri
Justin T. Cooper
Brian Dix
Aaron M. Dormaier
Lindsey Dudley
Brandi Good Bird
Austin Harrell
Ben Robert Herodes
Andrea C. Kelly
Casey Kern
David LaBoon
Matthew C. Langenfeld V
Melisa A. Larsen
Danielle LeMaster
Zachary K. Lowry

Mrs. Kline's class—Sioux chapter authors

Ron Horn

Ms. Glapion's class—Yakama chapter authors

INDEX

Kidding Around Series
Family Travel Guides

All are 7"x 9", 64 pages, and $9.95 paperback except for *Kidding Around the National Parks* and *Kidding Around Spain*, which are 108 pages and $12.95.
Kidding Around Atlanta, 2nd ed.
Kidding Around Boston, 2nd ed.
Kidding Around Chicago, 2nd ed.
Kidding Around the Hawaiian Islands
Kidding Around London, 2nd ed.
Kidding Around Los Angeles
**Kidding Around the National Parks
 of the Southwest**
Kidding Around New York City, 2nd ed.
Kidding Around Paris, 2nd ed.
Kidding Around Philadelphia
Kidding Around San Diego
Kidding Around San Francisco
Kidding Around Santa Fe
Kidding Around Seattle
Kidding Around Spain
Kidding Around Washington, D.C., 2nd ed.

X-ray Vision Series

Each title in the series is 8½" x 11", 48 pages, and $9.95 paperback, with four-color photographs and illustrations. All are written by Ron Schultz.
Looking Inside the Brain
Looking Inside Cartoon Animation
Looking Inside Caves and Caverns
Looking Inside Sports Aerodynamics
Looking Inside Sunken Treasure
**Looking Inside Telescopes and the
 Night Sky**

Masters of Motion Series

Each title in the series is 10¼" x 9", 48 pages, and $9.95 paperback, with four-color photographs and illustrations.
How to Drive an Indy Race Car
How to Fly a 747
How to Fly the Space Shuttle

Rainbow Warrior Artists Series

Each title is written by Reavis Moore with a foreword by LeVar Burton and is 8½" x 11", 48 pages, $14.95 hardcover and $9.95 paperback, with color photographs and illustrations.
Native Artists of Africa
Native Artists of Europe
Native Artists of North America

Extremely Weird Series

All of the titles are written by Sarah Lovett, 8½" x 11", 48 pages, $9.95 paperback and $14.95 hardcover.
Extremely Weird Bats
Extremely Weird Birds
Extremely Weird Endangered Species
Extremely Weird Fishes
Extremely Weird Frogs
Extremely Weird Insects
Extremely Weird Mammals
Extremely Weird Micro Monsters
Extremely Weird Primates
Extremely Weird Reptiles
Extremely Weird Sea Creatures
Extremely Weird Snakes
Extremely Weird Spiders

Kids Explore Series

Each title is written by kids, for kids, by the Westridge Young Writers Workshop, 7" x 9", with photographs and illustrations by the kids.
**Kids Explore America's African
 American Heritage**
 128 pages, $9.95 paperback
**Kids Explore America's Hispanic
 Heritage**
 112 pages, $9.95 paperback
**Kids Explore America's Japanese
 American Heritage**
 144 pages, $9.95 paperback
**Kids Explore the Gifts of Children With
 Special Needs**
 128 pages, $9.95 paperback

Bizarre & Beautiful Series

Each title is 8½" x 11", 48 pages, $9.95 paperback and $14.95 hardcover, with four-color photographs and illustrations.
Bizarre & Beautiful Ears
Bizarre & Beautiful Eyes
Bizarre & Beautiful Feelers
Bizarre & Beautiful Noses
Bizarre & Beautiful Tongues

Rough and Ready Series

Each title is 48 pages, 8½" x 11", and $12.95 hardcover, with two-color illustrations and duotone archival photographs.
Rough and Ready Cowboys
Rough and Ready Homesteaders
Rough and Ready Loggers
Rough and Ready Outlaws and Lawmen
Rough and Ready Prospectors
Rough and Ready Railroaders

American Origins Series

Each title is 48 pages, 8½" x 11", $12.95 hardcover, with two-color illustrations and duotone archival photographs.
Tracing Our English Roots
Tracing Our German Roots
Tracing Our Irish Roots
Tracing Our Italian Roots
Tracing Our Japanese Roots
Tracing Our Jewish Roots
Tracing Our Polish Roots

Environmental Titles

Habitats: Where the Wild Things Live
8½" x 11", 48 pages, color illustrations, $9.95 paper

**The Indian Way: Learning to
 Communicate with Mother Earth**
7" x 9", 114 pages, two-color illustrations, $9.95 paper

**Rads, Ergs, and Cheeseburgers: The Kids
 Guide to Energy and the Environment**
7" x 9", 108 pages, two-color illustrations, $13.95 paper

**The Kids' Environment Book: What's
 Awry and Why**
7" x 9",192 pages, two-color illustrations, $13.95 paper